5-20-76

The Medievalism of Victor Hugo

The Pennsylvania
State University
Studies No. 39

The Medievalism of Victor Hugo

by Patricia A. Ward

The Pennsylvania State University Press
University Park and London

Cover illustration: drawing by Victor Hugo

Library of Congress Cataloging in Publication Data

Ward, Patricia A   1940–
   The medievalism of Victor Hugo.

   (The Pennsylvania State University studies; no. 39)
   Bibliography: p. 126
   1. Hugo, Victor Marie, comte, 1802–1885 — Knowledge —
History. 2. Middle Ages in literature. I. Title. II. Series:
Pennsylvania. State University. The Pennsylvania State University
studies; no. 39.
PQ2304.H5W3   848'.7'09   74-28421
ISBN 0-271-01182-3

Designed by Glenn Ruby

Printed in the United States of America

Contents

1919338

Acknowledgment

Research for this study was made possible by a Fulbright Fellowship and a grant-in-aid from the Research Foundation of the State University of New York.

1

Introduction

In 1862, an edition of drawings by Victor Hugo was published in which Théophile Gautier describes Hugo: "Le poète possède cet oeil vision-naire dont il parle à propos d'Albert Dürer; il voit les choses par leur angle bizarre, & la vie cachée sous les formes se révèle à lui dans son activité mystérieuse."[1] Hugo, the poet-visionary, could have been an equally great painter; his imaginative powers enable him to animate nature, and, like Piranesi, "il aime à se promener dans les décombres des édifices abandonnés, à descendre les escaliers chancelants qui mènent aux lieux profonds, à errer dans le dédale obscur des couloirs sans issue, la lanterne sourde d'Anne Radcliffe à la main." Further, Gautier notes that "everyone" has read and reread *Notre-Dame de Paris;* it saved the art of the Middle Ages in France and gave to architecture a lyric impulse.

Gautier, in describing Hugo's artistic powers, makes specific refer-ence to Hugo's interest in the Middle Ages. Hugo was fascinated by the world of picturesque ruins popularized by the gothic novel; he actively promoted the restoration of the architectural monuments of France's medieval past; *Notre-Dame de Paris* was the most widely read work in France connected with the "curious malady"[2] of the craze for the gothic; and Hugo saw himself and was seen by others as a kind of Dante-Dürer — a visionary seer, transforming the inanimate world through his imaginative powers, while writing poetry and prose of political import. In short, Hugo's reputation in his own time was connected with the medieval revival in France. On the other hand, it has been maintained in the twentieth century that "Hugo did not really like the middle ages. He admired Gothic art and romantic ruins and stood in awe before the genius and energy of Charlemagne, Bar-barossa, Dante, John Huss, but he hated medieval obscurantism: 'J'aime la cathédrale et non le moyen âge' [*Les Quatre Vents de l'esprit,* livre satirique 29]."[3] This generalization accurately describes Hugo's ideas during part of his career, but it conceals both the complexity of the medieval revival in the nineteenth century, particularly in France, and the medievalism of Hugo himself.

Histories of literature frequently discuss Romantic interest in the Middle Ages. For instance, Paul Van Tieghem, in *Le Romantisme dans*

1

la littérature européenne, contrasts the "interior elements" of Romanticism (those connected with the "Romantic soul") with its "external elements" (those related to cultural taste and the relation of the individual to the world outside the self). Interest in the Middle Ages forms part of the latter category as evidence of the attempt of historically conscious Romantics to recapture their past.[4] For Van Tieghem, a trait common to the various manifestations of Romanticism was the abolition of the general prejudice against the Middle Ages that had been inherited from the age of classicism. Especially in Germany, a Christian, chivalric, virtuous medieval period replaced heroic Greece as the attempt was made to evoke and recreate a national past. Historians approached the Middle Ages in a new spirit, painting the past in vivid colors: Barante, in his *Histoire des ducs de Bourgogne,* tried to follow the chroniclers "dans le détail vivant des faits et des moeurs, de façon à offrir au lecteur le récit le plus concret et coloré possible, sans intervention critique ou philosophique du narrateur."[5] But even during the age of Romanticism, there was a reaction against the cult of the Middle Ages and a corresponding interest in other sources of the exotic, notably the Orient.[6]

Scholars have almost consistently viewed Romantic medievalism first as the continuation of pre-Romantic interest in the picturesque, national heritages, and chivalric ideals and also as evidence of conservative reaction to the excesses of the French Revolution and to a rapidly changing social order. In Germany, and then in England, the importance of medievalism for the politically conservative Romantics (and, later, the Victorians) was that "the partly historical and basically mythical Middle Ages . . . became a metaphor both for a specific social order and, somewhat more vaguely, for a metaphysically harmonious world view."[7] Although pre-Romantic trends in French medievalism continued during the first quarter of the nineteenth century, the movement from conservatism to liberalism in politics among the Romantics of Hugo's generation was marked. The Middle Ages could not be a metaphor for a golden age to which most of these French Romantics wished to return because their interpretation of history was dominated by the concept of progress, by a belief in an apocalyptic future, and by the advent of socialism.

In his preface to *Hernani* in 1830, Hugo proclaimed that literary freedom is the daughter of political freedom and that a literature of the people should succeed a literature of the court. His later statements about the relationship between Romanticism and politics became more forceful but did not essentially change. As a result, during the exile years, we find Hugo stating that "Romantisme, Socialisme, ce sont les pseudonymes du dix-neuvième siècle. Ce sont, en littérature et en politique, ses deux noms."[8] How then are we to reconcile the nineteenth-century view of Hugo as a participant in the medieval revival with the twentieth-century statement that he did not like the Middle Ages? And how are we to reconcile the more general views of Romantic medievalism as a metaphor for an ideal golden past to which political conservatives wished to revert with Hugo's statements, representing a generation of French Romantics, that Romanticism was synonymous with liberalism? These contradictions can be resolved by revising our ideas of the relationship between medievalism and Romanticism in general and by discovering how Hugo's transformation of medieval values reflects the functioning of his creative mind.

Romanticism was a European phenomenon of international scope from the late eighteenth century until approximately 1850. During this period the response to rapid political, social, economic and philosophical changes surrounding the French Revolution and industrialization produced a striking unity in the basic *Weltanschauung* of western Europe and ushered in the modern era. By this world view I mean "not a mere nexus of causes" but "an organic system, a cultural selfhood with a logic and autonomy of its own."[9] Because of this cultural selfhood, we can, in fact, speak of "the European mind,"[10] an ideal construct of basic attitudes which reveals the new orientation of western Europe within the historical period in question. How and when these attitudes became apparent varied from nation to nation, but examples can be drawn from most of western Europe. Although historians of French literature tend to emphasize the originality of French Romanticism,[11] or to discuss it with few references to other national literatures, it shared in this European *Weltanschauung,* even though its chronology differed significantly from that of England and Germany.

Since A.O. Lovejoy's important essay "On the Discrimination of Romanticisms," in which he indicates that there were numerous Romanticisms in Europe,[12] many critics and historians — from René Wellek, to Jacques Barzun, to Morse Peckham — have responded by attempting to describe a single European Romanticism. Whatever common denominators they may have found within Romanticism, they have assumed, at least implicitly, the ideal construct of a "European mind." Similarly, they have refrained from compiling catalogues of traits common to Romantic literature or art,[13] in favor of describing the underlying attitudes, metaphors, or assumptions of the period. Without developing a comprehensive theory of Romanticism, it is possible to isolate the European attitudes that underlie the medieval revival and show that Romantic medievalism was a manifestation of the fundamental changes in the European consciousness in the late eighteenth and early nineteenth centuries. Borrowing a linguistic concept and using it in a different context, we may say that a deep structure (an attitude or set of attitudes, sometimes consciously expressed and sometimes inarticulated) became transformed (manifested culturally), and Romantic medievalism was precisely such a manifestation.

One of these fundamental ideas, illustrating the cohesiveness of both Romantic literature and philosophy, was the positing of the thinking, feeling Self, and perhaps no one gave a more succinct expression to this new way of perceiving the individual and his relation to the outer world than did Byron in his dramatic poem *Manfred*. In act III, scene 4, Manfred demonstrates the ultimate power of the *Ich* when he exclaims to the last Spirit that appears to him:

> I bear within
> A torture which could nothing gain from thine:
> The mind which is immortal makes itself
> Requital for its good or evil thoughts, —
> Is its own origin of ill and end —
> And its own place and time. . . .

> (127–32)

Not only does Byron's character suggest that Mind is ultimate reality, but he expresses the inherent danger of solipsism, a danger the Romantics themselves acknowledged. The "torture" also indicates a felt disharmony — a sense of inner division or isolation — which he sees no way to overcome. Other Romantics expressed a similar feeling of isolation, but they often viewed it as a disharmony with their present world, and they sought ways to overcome their sense of dislocation. For them, the Self existed within society in the dynamic process of history.

Hugo's *Hernani* illustrates this sense of personal dislocation within history. The two male protagonists, Hernani and Don Carlos, are projections of these basic ideas about the Self within society and in time. First, Hernani, the dispossessed and doomed, calls himself a *proscrit*, robbed by the monarchy of his rightful noble identity, and by the aged Don Ruy Gomez, of Doña Sol. Second, Don Carlos, during his famous monologue before the tomb of Charlemagne in act IV, comes to an almost visionary awareness of his role as an agent to provide unity for society and a new way of life for the oppressed. It is he who can give back to Hernani his true identity and end his isolation. In this scene, Hugo portrays the unity of medieval society as stemming from the enlightened offices of the Holy Roman Emperor and the Pope — "ces deux moitiés de Dieu." The solidarity of the social edifice can continue only as the needs of the masses are met; this is Hugo's message to the nineteenth century and, in turn, Don Carlos's own recognition within the time sequence of the play. "Rois! regardez en bas!/ — Ah! le peuple! — océan! — onde sans cesse émue" (1536–37). The choice of a medieval motif to suggest that unity can be achieved for both the masses and the individual within a stable political order indicates that in 1829 and 1830 the Middle Ages were a metaphor for Hugo's own desire to overcome the disharmony he sensed in French society, particularly during a period of unrest that culminated in the popular uprisings of the July Revolution.

This example leads to the much broader hypothesis that medievalism was essentially a sign of the search by many Romantics for a society in which the complete integration of the individual would be possible. The nineteenth-century view of history was complex; for political conservatives and liberals (and the religiously orthodox and unorthodox) the Middle Ages became a metaphor signifying different aspects of this single underlying dissatisfaction with the relation between the individual and society. The complexity of the medieval revival is in the Romantics' vision of the past and future. "Romanticism represents a new tendency to see a positive value and interest in civilizations very different from its own. This, by itself, might develop into a futile nostalgia for the past, a desire, for example, to bring back the Middle Ages; but actually that development was checked by the presence in Romanticism of another conception, viz., the conception of history as progress, a development of human reason or the education of mankind."[14]

Medievalism was assimilated into nineteenth-century historicism in its true sense — the appreciation of the past and the belief that history was a dynamic process, the idea that society was progressing toward freedom and, at its extreme, that an apocalypse was almost at hand. As they became increasingly liberal, many Romantics, and Hugo was one of them, developed an ambivalent attitude toward the Middle Ages, which both fascinated and repelled them. But for others, the medieval period remained a positive ideal, a metaphor for a conservative social order. Consequently, a "positive" and a "negative" medievalism can be distinguished within Romanticism.[15] Those who saw the period in a positive light emphasized the historical distance between past and present, desiring to return to the past. Those with a more ambivalent attitude also were aware of this separation between past and present, but they were more concerned with the future because the future promised a revolutionary change. The medieval past, as part of the historical process, was of interest: its political and religious institutions were largely rejected, but those elements in its imaginative art and culture which paralleled nineteenth-century taste were admired.

This relationship between the medieval revival in its positive and negative elements and the historical consciousness of the nineteenth century is clarified by a comparison of texts on chivalry. In the eighteenth century there had already been some learned interest in chivalry, stirred primarily by La Curne de Sainte-Palaye's *Mémoires sur l'ancienne chevalerie* which helped to popularize the chivalric ideal. Chateaubriand used Sainte-Palaye as a major source for his idealized discussion of chivalry in the *Génie du christianisme* (pt. 4, bk. 5) where he sees the qualities of the *chevalier* as creating a "tableau de . . . vertus chrétiennes." Walter Scott, partly under the influence of Goethe's *Götz von Berlichingen,* repeats this ideal when he has Ivanhoe exclaim that "the pure light of chivalry . . . raises us victorious over pain, toil, and suffering, and teaches us to fear no evil but disgrace." Chivalry is "the nurse of pure and high affection, the stay of the oppressed, the redresser of grievances, the curb of the power of the tyrant." And in *Quentin Durward,* Scott sets up a contrast between chivalric and utilitarian society (the past and the present) through the characters of Quentin Durward and Louis XI.[16] Scott recognizes that during the medieval period oppression and tyranny existed, but emphasizes the power of chivalry to protect the oppressed and has no sympathy with revolution or insurgency.

By the time that Hugo wrote "La terre a vu jadis errer des paladins" in the 1850s for the section "Les Chevaliers errants" of *La Légende des Siècles,* a subtle change in emphasis had come about, both in the portrait of the *chevalier* and in the portrayal of the Middle Ages as an era of oppression. The darkness of the medieval world now becomes palpable and the *chevalier* is transformed into a gigantic force, flashing like lightning in this backward era.

> Ils étaient, dans des temps d'oppression, de deuil,
> De honte, où l'infamie étalait son orgueil,
> Les spectres de l'honneur, du droit, de la justice.[17]

Although one might conclude that the intensity of the imagery of Hugo's poem is the result of the political stance of his exile years and is post-Romantic, the themes of this poem appear to be a continuation of attitudes already present in *Hernani* and *Notre-Dame de Paris.* In *Hernani,* Don Carlos wishes to embody the qualities of a Charlemagne in order to save the structure of a society in which the masses have begun to stir. Unlike Scott's *Quentin Durward,* which Hugo had read, *Notre-Dame de Paris* reveals a sympathy for popular uprisings and for the *peuple* in general.[18] But the themes of *Hernani* and *Notre-Dame* become combined in later years once the Middle Ages are part of a broad historical vision. In *La Légende des Siècles,* therefore, nineteenth-century historicism is at work as Hugo looks at progress within civilization, revealing his own faith in an apocalyptic future. The *chevalier* comes to represent a gleam of progress within the otherwise bleak medieval period. This ambivalent use of medieval motifs is an excellent example of "negative" medievalism.

Hugo's interest in the Middle Ages and his embodiment of this interest in literary form are directly related both to his own political and religious evolution and to his perception of his role in the nineteenth century. He began his career by sharing the general Romantic feeling of being at odds with the established order of his world and by trying to achieve integration and reform society. His literary use of medieval material illustrates both his relation to Romanticism and important aspects of Romanticism as a movement. But Hugo moved beyond the attitudes of the 1820s and 1830s, and he increasingly personalized his use of medieval material; after the days of the medieval revival that he helped to instigate, the medieval period was still a metaphor for Hugo's social and religious attitudes, but the medieval allusions became fewer and fewer, and his general attitude toward the period was ever more hostile. Yet, his literary use of medieval motifs and allusions was increasingly stamped by the genius of his poetic force. The most significant aspect of a study of Hugo's literary use of medieval material does not lie, as a result, in the themes or ideas for which he created metaphors. He did not have a great many original things to say about the Middle Ages, especially since he did not know many of the chronicles or much of the literature first hand and was not influenced by the rise of medieval scholarship in the nineteenth century. Hugo's assimilation of a few key elements from the medieval revival into his creative imagination which became constants to be reused in various combinations and the linguistic force of several of his works with medieval subject matter provide the fascinating material for study. Hugo's medievalism, when analyzed in its total evolution, is a vehicle toward understanding the functioning of his creative mind.

Hugo seems to have experimented with various literary genres in his use of medieval subject matter: with the novel in *Notre-Dame de Paris,* the drama in *Les Burgraves,* and the epic in *La Légende des Siècles,* not to mention various lyric poems, the "voyage" material which includes architectural and historical observations, especially in *Le Rhin,* and the recurring allusions that appear throughout his works. There are several broad patterns which become evident in the material as a whole. In the poetry and prose which are narrative, Hugo seems to have been looking for the proper form for his expansive descriptive powers. His personal identification with the great figures of the period shines through in his visionary works, especially when the Dante-Dürer-Hugo analogy is established as a fixed reference. Even in the late years when Hugo no longer wrote works that were "medieval," the vestiges of the medieval revival remain in his scattered references and allusions. Throughout the corpus of Hugo's works, the historical distance between the nineteenth century and the Middle Ages is apparent, for the analogy between the past and present is meant to exist in order that Hugo may cast light upon the problems of nineteenth-century culture. Even in *Notre-Dame de Paris* where the aim is to recreate and evoke fifteenth-century Paris and its architecture, Hugo the modern author intrudes to indicate why that architecture would disappear and have to be rescued and restored in the nineteenth century. The Middle Ages form a past which can be recaptured only to serve the present.

2

Hugo and the Rise of Medievalism in France

Although Hugo was one of the figures in French culture responsible for the widespread interest in gothic architecture during the 1830s, he and other Romantics of his generation were by no means the first to depict the Middle Ages in a more favorable light than had predecessors for whom the term "gothic" was synonymous with "barbaric" and "crude." Hugo grew up in an atmosphere of curiosity about the past fostered by scholars of the Enlightenment. Pre-Romantic sensibility also had led to a portrait of a picturesque era, and a trend of popular culture resulted which no doubt influenced his early interest in the Middle Ages.[1]

A changing philosophy of history and method of writing history had characterized the *philosophes*, who studied their sources critically and looked upon the culture of previous ages as a unity. Their attitude toward history was shared by other eighteenth-century erudites, notably the *robe* scholars connected with the Académie des Inscriptions et Belles-Lettres. Curiosity about the Middle Ages was common in this group, for, as political conservatives, but also as representatives of the modern spirit, they wanted to link the nobility of the Middle Ages to the eighteenth-century French aristocracy.[2] The most notable medievalist of this group was La Curne de Sainte-Palaye, whose most influential work was the *Mémoires sur l'ancienne chevalerie*, first given as a series of lectures from 1746 to 1750. The *Mémoires* became "the principal source from which writers and historians took their information and in some cases their ideas about chivalry."[3] Misunderstanding the historical development of chivalry, Sainte-Palaye interpreted it as a creation of the monarchy and therefore used this medieval institution to support and justify the *ancien régime*. He delighted in the picturesque in chivalry; it coincided with his taste and was appealing to nineteenth-century taste in general.[4] As noted earlier, Chateaubriand based many of his remarks in the *Génie du christianisme* on Sainte-Palaye's portrayal of the chivalric ideal. Charles Nodier published a new edition of Sainte-Palaye in 1826, and probably Hugo's own long-standing interest in the *chevalier,* so important in *La Légende des Siècles,* can be traced through Nodier and Chateaubriand to Sainte-Palaye.

Sainte-Palaye was the most outstanding of a number of scholars whose historical interest caused them to discover the Middle Ages and edit works of the period, but they were not noticeably sympathetic, which is understandable given Enlightenment attitudes. Sainte-Palaye, for instance, could say "que peut-on attendre des Siècles ténébreux dont j'entreprends de retracer l'image."[5] Yet, in preparing *Han d'Islande* and *Notre-Dame de Paris,* Hugo made use of some of this eighteenth-century scholarship, particularly Mallet's *Introduction à l'histoire de Dannemarc* (1755), a breakthrough in eighteenth-century historiography according to Meinecke, Sauval's *Histoire et recherches des antiquités de la ville de Paris* (1724), and the Lenglet-Dufresnoy edition of the *Mémoires de Commynes* (1747).[6] Hugo may also have known the Lenglet-Defresnoy edition of the *Roman de la Rose,*[7] and he certainly knew Rivarol's translation of Dante's *Inferno.*[8] Paradoxically he did not draw to any extent on the scholarship of nineteenth-century figures such as Barante, Sismondi, Raynouard, and, later, Guizot, Fauriel, and Ampère. When he did use sources, he did so uncritically as in his use of a popular article by Achille Jubinal for the "Mariage de Roland," "Aymerillot," and "L'Aigle du casque" of *La Légende des Siècles,*[9] but then Hugo's primary concern was not total accuracy.

Throughout the eighteenth century, popular tradition, aristocratic society, and even major writers and composers fostered an interest in chivalry and chivalric romance. *Amadis of Gaul* and *Jerusalem Delivered* were both read, but Voltaire's *Tancrède* (1760), Gluck's *Armide* (1777), and Grétry's *Richard Coeur de Lion* (1784) indicate the importance of the chivalric theme. The *Bibliothèque Bleue* was successful in circulating versions of chivalric romances among the public as was the *Bibliothèque universelle des romans* after 1775 for a more aristocratic audience. The adaptations of the Comte de Tressan for the latter were not critical, to say the least, and the tone was "uniformément celui d'une assez fade galanterie, relevée çà et là de libertinage."[10]

By 1800 a new literary form, the "genre troubadour," resulted from all this interest in chivalry and romance, but writers like Millevoye were really creating narrative ballads which were pastiches of archaisms, chivalric themes, and troubadour "commonplaces." They had no knowledge, essentially, of medieval poetry. Again, serial publication formed popular taste, and the *Almanach des Muses, Almanach des Dames,* and *Almanach des Muses dédié aux Dames* were the chief purveyors of this poetry.[11] It has been claimed that the genre troubadour lay behind the *ballade* form that Hugo was to use in the 1820s; in any case, as a boy

Hugo was not immune to the troubadour vogue, for one of his earliest poems, "Richard Coeur de Lion," is written on the theme of the *trouvère* Blondel coming to the aid of the imprisoned Richard.

Chateaubriand's *Génie du christianisme* appeared in 1802 during the vogue for chivalry and troubadour poetry, but his portrayal of the Middle Ages stems from a different personal sensibility. Of the impact this book had on French society, he could claim in his 1828 preface that "les Français apprirent à porter avec regret leur regard sur le passé; les voies de l'avenir furent préparées, et des espérances presque éteintes se ranimèrent."[12] Out of his own conservatism, sensibility to changes brought about by the French Revolution, and, perhaps, *mal du siècle,* Chateaubriand described a Christian ideal incarnate in the codes of chivalry and the gothic cathedral, of which vestiges remained in the nineteenth century. Echoing the elegiac tone of both Ossianic poetry[13] and Volney's *Les Ruines,* Chateaubriand created a world of picturesque ruins, a world no more like that of the Middle Ages than that of the pseudo-medieval genre troubadour; his descriptions underscore the historical distance between present and past, especially when he speaks of the ruins of Christian monuments. "Il n'est aucune ruine d'un effet plus pittoresque que ces débris: . . . leur architecture gothique a quelque chose de grand et sombre, comme le Dieu de Sinaï, dont elle perpetue le souvenir. . . . Le vent circule dans les ruines, et leurs innombrables jours deviennent autant de tuyaux d'où s'échappent des plaintes; l'orgue avait jadis moins de soupirs sous ces voûtes religieuses."[14] No better example could be given of the element of the picturesque (and Chateaubriand himself speaks of the "effet pittoresque des ruines") as it became associated with the architecture of the Middle Ages, colored by the nostalgic regret of the observer of the scene. For a time, this picturesque world was more important to the young Hugo than any remarks Chateaubriand may have made about the *frisson* produced in him by the gothic cathedral or the parallel between the primitive forests of Gaul and the vaults of the cathedral (pt. 3, bk. 1).[15]

Adèle Hugo's description of the effect of the *Génie du christianisme* on her husband is well known. "Victor accepta peu à peu cette croyance qui se confondait avec l'architecture des cathédrales et avec les grandes images de la Bible, et passa du royalisme voltairien de sa mère au royalisme chrétien de Chateaubriand."[16] Chateaubriand's influence is obvious in the general tenor of Hugo's conservative politics after 1819, and the older literary figure dominated the *Conservateur littéraire,* the review Hugo and his brother Abel published from 1819 to 1821, to such an extent that it has been called the "conservateur de Chateaubriand."[17] Allusions to Chateaubriand are evident in the *Odes,* especially between 1819 and 1824,[18] but at this time Hugo's reading did not lead him to portray the Middle Ages as Christian or to view gothic architecture as symbolic of the infinite. Not until after his acquaintance with Nodier and the Baron von Eckstein did Hugo voice these ideas or become truly caught up in the medieval revival that centered around architecture.[19] All the same, Chateaubriand instilled in Hugo a response to medieval ruins that was to become vital to the latter's creative vision, especially after the voyages on the Rhine. Hugo's intense response to ruins is already apparent when he describes the *château* at Dreux in a letter to Vigny in 1821. "Ces ruines m'ont plu. Figurez-vous, sur une colline haute et escarpée, de vieilles tours de cailloux noyés dans la chaux, décrenelées, inégales, et liées ensemble par de gros pans de mur où le temps a fait encore plus de brèches que les assauts."[20]

Although Chateaubriand's poetic defense of Christianity idealized the Middle Ages and contributed to the medieval vogue in the early nineteenth century, several other works set the pace for Hugo. Madame de Staël's *De l'Allemagne* brought German literature to Hugo.[21] The well-known passages in which she defines the Germanic spirit, distinguishes between "classic" and "romantic," and points to German enthusiasm for the Middle Ages enforced and expanded the interest already aroused in Hugo.[22]

Although August Wilhelm Schlegel's lectures on dramatic literature (*Cours de littérature dramatique*) were published in the translation of Madame Necker de Saussure in 1814, Hugo did not know much about Schlegel's ideas regarding the Middle Ages and Romantic theory until about 1825 or 1826 and may never have read Schlegel himself. *De l'Allemagne* would have been the first intermediary by which Hugo learned of the Schlegel brothers. Madame de Staël's interest in northern mythology may have stimulated Hugo's use of motifs from Scandinavian mythology and a Scandinavian setting for *Han d'Islande*.[23] She describes the shadowy world of the North where "tout semble donner l'idée d'un espace inconnu, d'un univers nocturne dont notre monde est environné" and enthusiastically endorses the plays of the Danish writer Oehlenschläger.[24]

Several other works known to Hugo contributed to the medieval vogue during the Restoration. Marchangy's *La Gaule poétique* soon went through six editions after it was published in 1813. Influenced by Chateaubriand, Marchangy created a prose epic on the national origins of France. Among his goals were to explore "la vie privée de nos devanciers"; to examine "leurs ruines, leurs tombeaux, les débris de leurs législations primitives et barbares, les oracles de leurs cultes sauvages et toutes leurs institutions féodales, guerrières, super-stitieuses, chevaleresques ou galantes"; and to extract from the litera-ture of the Middle Ages treasures which could be appreciated by the poet, annalist, legislator, and archeologist.[25] The work is a combination of historical and supernatural elements; it centers on Charlemagne, but its characters include fairies and ogres.[26] Charlemagne is portrayed as the consummate hero who was responsible for an enlightenment during the dark ages, as well as for the birth of France. "De même qu'un phare placé au milieu des ténèbres, pour rallier à sa lumière les nations turbulentes et barbares, Charlemagne s'élève au-dessus de ses prédécesseurs, de ses contemporains, de ses descendants."[27]

This imagery and hyperbole, absorbed by Hugo from the general culture of the Restoration, reinforced his interest in the heroic figure of light within the shadowy Middle Ages. In 1837, during the medieval revival connected with the gothic, Sainte-Beuve commented on the taste for a pseudo-medieval period evident during the first quarter of the century: "C'était le temps de la mode d'Ossian et d'un Charlemagne enjolivé, le temps de la fausse Gaule poétique bien avant Thierry, des Scandinaves bien avant les cours d'Ampère, et la ballade avant Victor Hugo."[28]

Interest in the preservation of the antiquities of France was actively promoted by learned societies and by the publication between 1820 and 1840 of *Voyages pittoresques et romantiques dans l'ancienne France* of Nodier, Taylor, and Cailleux. The first volume of the *Voyages pittoresques* lay behind Hugo's 1823 ode "La Bande noire" in which he pleads for the preservation of the monuments of the past; Hugo's descriptions of the picturesque in the poem parallel at various points the lithographs of the *Voyages,* and the book "played moreover an important part in introducing Hugo to the fascination of medieval buildings seen in the context of popular legends and historical anecdotes."[29] Further, "popular" poetry, long a part of Germany's evocation of her national past, began to supersede in importance the epics that continued to be written even as the classic-romantic debate began to rage in France. Abel Hugo's translation of Spanish romances appeared in 1822, preceded by an essay, "Discours sur la poésie historique chantée, et sur la romance espagnole," which was a compilation of extracts from the course on Spanish literature given at the Société des Bonnes Lettres in 1821. Hugo locates these romances, or "chansons historiques et religieuses," in oral tradition, gives a brief survey, with extracts, of the different poems, and concludes that the romance was of primary importance in Spain but remained secondary in France.[30]

By 1822 when Hugo began to write *Han d'Islande,* many forces within France had molded his conception of a picturesque medieval world which he associated with the images of heroic romance and chivalry and of isolated ruins located on a rugged landscape. Although the immediate sources for this first novel were England and the North, some of the literary models had been popular in France for a long time. Macpherson's forgeries of Ossian, popularized by translations like that of Le Tourneur during the late eighteenth century, were especially influential during the Empire. Scandinavian mythology was discovered almost simultaneously; in fact, the two worlds of Ossian and the *Edda*s were constantly confused in the eighteenth century.[31] Mallet's treatment of Scandinavian civilization in his history of Denmark and his translations of passages from the *Edda*s were extremely important in disseminating knowledge of northern mythology.[32]

The plan and first act of a tragedy, *Athélie ou Les Scandinaves* (1817), indicate that *Han d'Islande* was not Hugo's first attempt to use northern antiquities in his writings. Although the setting is the temple of Odin in the sacred wood of Tornstan, the play is written in the style of classical tragedy. "Promenade Nocturne," a poem written in the same year, reflects to a greater degree the landscape of the post-Chateaubriand, Ossianic poetic conventions as the poet describes his feelings before the shadowy world of medieval ruins.

> Que vois-je? quelles sont ces ruines antiques,
> > Ces vieux créneaux, ces vastes tours,
> Et ces vitraux brisés, et ces porches gothiques,
> Et ces murs dont la lune argente les contours?[33]

Hugo subtitled "Les Derniers Bardes" (1819) a "poème ossianique"; it is based on the invasion of Scotland by Edward I and consists of a condemnation by the bards of the English king. "Vous ne reviendrez plus, beaux jours, siècles prospères!" — "Vous êtes les bourreaux, nous sommes les victimes," cry the poets, stating two themes which were often reworked by Hugo (*Oeuvres poétiques*, 1: 163 and 167).

Hugo also drew upon the vogue for gothic horror and Walter Scott in his preparation of *Han*. Jean-Bertrand Barrère has pointed out that Maturin, Anne Radcliffe, and "Monk" Lewis from England, in addition to Tieck from Germany, were especially significant in this vogue. "Charles Nodier, leur introducteur en France, faisait liaison entre la tradition française illustrée par Cazotte . . . et les apports de l'étranger."[34] Nodier's adaptations of the *Vampire* (1820) and *Bertram* (1821) and his own *Jean Sbogar* (1818) and *Smarra* (1821) were undoubtedly known by Hugo, who cites *Bertrand* several times in the epigraphs of the novel. At the same time, Hugo consciously followed Walter Scott. He called the novel a long drama in which the scenes were tableaux of description, decorations, and costumes, and in which characters created themselves through their dialogue. "Du reste, tous les personnages se peignaient par eux-mêmes; c'était une idée que les compositions de Walter Scott m'avaient inspirée et que je voulais tenter dans l'intérêt de notre littérature. Je passai beaucoup de temps à amasser pour ce roman des matériaux historiques et géographiques, et plus de temps encore à en mûrir la conception, à en disposer les masses, à en combiner les détails."[35] The result of welding together these traditions was a "roman fantastique à structure historique."[36]

The setting of *Han d'Islande* is Norway, and the political intrigue and miners' revolt which surround the imprisoned Schumacker, former grand-chancellor who has been betrayed by the current grand-chancellor d'Ahlefeld, occur in 1699. But a set of characters who, in a sense, do not exist in time is placed in this geographically and histori-cally documented world. On the one hand, we find Ordener Gulden-lew and Ethel, Schumacker's daughter, the hero and heroine types of romance.[37] (Ordener has vowed to recover a lost box of papers which prove the innocence of Schumacker, and he eventually marries Ethel.) On the other hand, there are three grotesque figures: Han, a monster-bandit who Ordener assumes has the box and whom he goes seeking, Spiagudry, the keeper of the morgue, who accompanies Ordener on part of his quest, and Nychol Orugix, the hangman. The relationship between Ethel and Ordener was inspired by the young Hugo's feelings for Adèle Foucher, and the action of the novel is usually recounted from the point of view of Ordener. His sensibility and emotional responses undoubtedly jar the twentieth-century reader, but Hugo treats his hero with utmost seriousness. For instance, when Ordener, during his search for Han, glimpses in the distance the light of Munckholm where Ethel is imprisoned, the narrator comments that those who do not understand the happiness of Ordener at the moment are not destined to taste the true joys of life. "Tout son coeur se souleva de ravissement; son sein gonflé, palpitant avec force, re-spirait à peine. Immobile, l'oeil tendu, il contemplait l'astre de consola-tion et d'espérance."[38] Although Ordener may represent *le beau*, Han d'Islande, the forerunner of other Hugolian monster figures, is *le laid* in the kind of juxtaposition which Hugo later discussed in *La Préface de Cromwell*. Han, too, is described with gravity by the narrator in what Barrère has called "ce jeu sauvage."[39]

Perhaps as a result of this seriousness of tone, Hugo's preface of 1833 belittles *Han d'Islande* as a work of youth, nothing more than a "roman fantastique" whose aim was to terrify old ladies and small children. Nevertheless, several critics have interpreted the book as a parody centering about the figure of Spiagudry.[40] A garrulous man of erudition, Spiagudry is easily terrorized by the fantastic world of which he, as keeper of the morgue, is a part; he is an obvious comic figure. The hangman, Nichol Orugix, is parodied as the institution of the *bourreau* is mocked — in order to be destroyed.[41] But a search for parody soon leads to the discovery that the documentary tone of the geographical and historical world is put in question by Hugo himself in his very first preface. With tongue-in-cheek, he concludes that the anonymous author has given particular attention to the picturesque part of the novel.

> On y rencontre fréquemment des K, des Y, des H et des W, quoiqu'il n'ait jamais employé ces caractères romantiques qu'avec une extrême sobriété, témoin le nom historique de Guldenlew, que plusieurs chroniqueurs écrivent Guldenloëwe, ce qu'il n'a pas osé se permettre; . . . et qu'enfin tous les chapitres sont précédés d'épigraphes étranges et mystérieuses, qui ajoutent singulièrement à l'intérêt et donnent plus de physionomie à chaque partie de la composition. (PP. 5–6)

The first preface suggests that Hugo had some hesitations about the "roman fantastique" even in 1822, despite the fact that Ordener's excessive feeling may have been an expression of Hugo's own idyllic love at the time. The humor used in connection with the executioners contrasts to the serious tone of the whole, indicating that Hugo's conception of the novel may not have been unified.

Hugo's use of medieval motifs reinforces the tension in the design of the novel; there is no integration of the picturesque world of ruins, of the consciousness on the part of the narrator of past history and mythology, with the world of Schumacker, Ordener, and Han.[42] All these elements exist side by side without reinforcing one another except when Ordener's sensitive nature responds to the ruins he sees. An analysis of a representative passage will indicate what is meant. When Ordener climbs the ruins of Vermund le Proscrit, the narrator steps into the scene with a commentary.

> Que le lecteur ne s'étonne pas si nous rencontrons souvent des ruines à la cime des monts de Norvège. . . . En Norvège surtout, au siècle où nous nous sommes transportés, ces sortes de constructions aériennes étonnaient autant par leur variété que par leur nombre. . . . On voyait près des frêles arcades ogives d'un cloître gothique les lourds piliers égyptiens d'une église saxonne; près de la citadelle à tours carrées d'un chef payen, la forteresse à créneaux d'un sire chrétien; près d'un château-fort ruiné par le temps, un monastère détruit par la guerre. . . . Les traditions s'éteignent avec les ans, comme un feu qu'on n'a point recueilli; et qui pourrait ensuite pénétrer le secret des siècles? (PP. 156–57)

The narrator has broken into the sequence of events and has reaffirmed the historical distance between the nineteenth-century real world, the seventeenth-century fictive world, and the medieval past of that fictive world. The historical distance becomes so great with the passing of time that the Middle Ages cannot be recaptured in the novel. "Qui pourrait ensuite pénétrer le secret des siècles?"

The architectural flavor of the passage, though written in a third person, documentary tone, is in the tradition of Chateaubriand. The ruins of the manor of Vermund le Proscrit (p. 157) are derived from the remains of the Tour de Guy de la Roche-Guyon which Hugo visited in 1821. Although writing in a style "vif, pittoresque et plein de nerfs" according to Nodier, Hugo still clings to a conventional mode of expression. The seriousness of tone in all passages involving Ordener contrasts with the parodic aspects of the novel. Hugo indicated in his 1833 preface how this passage falls short when considered within the frame of the novel: the observation of the author had not yet matured and become yoked to an inspiration best suited to his self-expression.

The paucity of references to the age of Scandinavian mythology indicates that Hugo had not yet been totally swept up in the vogue for the Middle Ages, but writing the novel brought him in contact with the two men who were probably most responsible for focusing his attention on the Middle Ages, the Baron von Eckstein and Charles Nodier. Eckstein, a disciple of Friedrich Schlegel, wrote innumerable articles, diffusing German erudition and, more particularly, conservative Catholicism, Schlegelian literary theory, and knowledge of oriental and medieval literatures.[43] In 1823, he became director of the *Annales de la littérature et des arts,* mouthpiece for the Société des Bonnes Lettres and successor to the ill-starred *Conservateur littéraire.* Since both Abel and Victor Hugo were active in this society, they probably knew Eckstein at this time. In 1822, Eckstein published two brief extracts from the *Elder Edda,* the "Chant de Hnikar" and the "Chant de Fafnir."[44] Now in *Han d'Islande,* Hugo publishes two epigraphs, at the head of chapters 25 and 29, which appear to be taken from the "Chant de Fafnir," the second extract published by Eckstein. Since the *Annales* appeared while Hugo was writing *Han d'Islande,* the extracts no doubt caught his attention and were used for the epigraphs. Knowledge of their source and of the other reading by Hugo as he prepared the novel provides an ironic footnote for Nodier's review in the *Quotidienne* for 12 March 1823; he remarks that "on reconnaît d'ailleurs, dans *Han d'Islande,* une bonne lecture de l'Edda et de l'histoire, beaucoup d'érudition, beaucoup d'esprit."[45] After reading Nodier's remarks, Hugo sought him out to thank him, and a friendship resulted.

Nodier's influence on Hugo has been thoroughly studied; he has been attributed primarily with being a source for Hugo's interest in the grotesque and the fantastic.[46] However, in his poetry of 1823 and 1824, Hugo begins to link a *merveilleux* of *fées* and *sylphes* with the Middle Ages, incorporating these creatures into the troubadour tradition. The first three ballades, "Une Fée" (1824), "Le Sylphe" (1823), and "La Grand'mère," are written in the spirit both of the troubadour poems and of Nodier's *Smarra, Trilby,* and the *Fée aux Miettes.* The first two stanzas of "Une Fée" illustrate how Hugo expresses two aspects of the medieval vogue of the first quarter of the century, especially if they are compared with "Le Cor" by Vigny, written strictly in the troubadour tradition.

> Que ce soit Urgèle ou Morgane,
> J'aime, en un rêve sans effroi,
> Qu'une fée, au corps diaphane,
> Ainsi qu'une fleur qui se fane,
> Vienne pencher son front sur moi.
>
> C'est elle dont le luth d'ivoire
> Me redit, sur un mâle accord,
> Vos contes, qu'on n'oserait croire,
> Bons paladins, si votre histoire
> N'était plus merveilleuse encor.

> *(Oeuvres poétiques,* 1. 499)

Vigny, too, following the traditional subject matter of Roland's death at Roncevaux, uses the "luth du troubadour" in part three where the sense of well-being of Charlemagne and his troops contrasts to the sound of the horn at Roncevaux.

Elsewhere in the poetry of this period, Hugo recalls the figure of Roland as he reveals his own royalism in the 1823 ode, "La Guerre d'Espagne." "If faut, comme un soldat, qu'un prince ait une épée./ . . . On ne peut te briser, sceptre de Charlemagne,/ Sans briser le fer de Roland!" *(Oeuvres poétiques,* 1. 355). There is an enormous contrast between Hugo's view of chivalry as the right arm of the monarchy expressed here and in the "Chant du Tournoi" (1824) and that of *La Légende des Siècles* many years later.

Hugo's interest in architecture becomes more pronounced in the poetry of 1823–24, but he shows no specific knowledge of romanesque or gothic styles, and he uses the picturesque vocabulary he inherited from Chateaubriand (as in "Paysage"). Elsewhere, the "château de fées" is the image used to communicate the poet's fleeting moments of happiness (in "A G . . . Y."), and the *fée,* symbol of western tradition in "La Fée et la Péri," claims to rule over both "palais magiques" and "églises gothiques," In the well-known "La Bande noire," Hugo looks at medieval architecture as the monument of a "peuple enfant" and its ruins as the reminder of an age of chivalry. The poet's task is to sing of past glories in the face of the destructive anarchy of the present. At this point in his career Hugo, who used lithographs as a source for this particular poem, was not writing as a keen, informed observer of medieval architecture. He had inherited the conventions of a vogue.

Until the end of 1824, the Middle Ages attracted Hugo's attention, but not in a compelling way. The following year brought the beginnings of the romantic debate, friendship with Nodier, travels to Blois and the Alps — experiences significant for Hugo's artistic maturation. When Hugo became a first-hand observer of architectural monuments, he incorporated the Middle Ages into his *fantaisie* and found a nonconventional form for the expression of this medievalism.

3

The Years 1825 to 1828

The years 1825 to 1828, the period of Hugo's gradual conversion to the Romantic movement in literature and a more liberal stance in politics, also mark the consolidation of his interest in the Middle Ages. Compared with the vogue of the first part of the century, a vague approximation of the Middle Ages, the medieval revival of the 1820s and 1830s was clearly linked to a reordering of attitudes toward history, politics, literature, and architecture. In Germany the very term "Romantic" had earlier become synonymous with medieval literature, and the new aesthetic in art had been explained by an analogy with gothic architecture.

During the discussions of the 1820s in Paris, the definitions of the Schlegels surfaced once again. For example, the Baron von Eckstein wrote that historically "on peut appeler du nom *romantique* toute la littérature chevaleresque et chrétienne du moyen âge; la poésie romantique, dans son acceptation la plus générale, s'applique donc à l'état social des peuples de l'Europe germaine et latine du moyen âge."[1] He also explained that the Schlegel brothers established "un parallèle entre deux ordres d'architecture différens, celui qui régnait dans les temples de la Grèce, et celui qui a présidé à la construction des cathédrales du christianisme, auxquelles on donne le nom de gothique."[2]

Form dominates in the art of the ancients; the whole work aspires toward perfect beauty, toward "l'harmonie des parties." "L'âme, au contraire, règne dans l'art des modernes. Cet art, comme la religion dont il émane, tend vers l'infini."[3] In order, then, for the interest in the antiquities of medieval France to have a revolutionary impact on nineteenth-century culture, it had to extend beyond the crusade to preserve these monuments from destruction. Once medieval art was linked to an aesthetic of unity in variety, medievalism passed into new literary forms as part of the program of the Romantics.

Hugo's conversion to Romantic medievalism and the literary expression of this interest are of particular importance during the period 1825 to 1828. In the *Ballades,* he makes virtuoso use of the genre troubadour traditions while experimenting with poetic form, but in *La Préface de Cromwell,* he incorporates the Middle Ages and the variety seen by the Romantics in medieval art into his personal theory of the grotesque. The *ballades* of 1825 reveal not only a number of verse forms but also the entire medieval vogue which Hugo had inherited. The poetry of 1828, however, indicates more markedly his fascination with poetic form and his movement toward a poetic vision that would animate the architectural monuments of the past. In these works Hugo is not concerned with an accurate portrayal of the medieval period, though by 1828 he was already thinking about *Notre-Dame de Paris* and recreating the atmosphere of Louis XI's Paris.

Seven of the *ballades* were written between April and October of 1825, which has been called "l'année des *Ballades*."[4] The composition of the poems during this span of time seems to indicate that they were directly related to Hugo's travels. As early as 1893, Léopold Mabilleau recognized that the "latent" Romaniticism of Hugo was brought out by his trips during 1825 and that this Romanticism was to reveal itself in both his aesthetic doctrine and style.[5] Jean-Bertrand Barrère sees the voyages, especially those made later with Juliette Drouet, as the key factor in the development of Hugo's imagination.[6] In particular, Hugo's taste for medieval architecture seems to have been whetted by his visits to Blois in April, Reims in May, the Alps in August, and Montfort-l'Amaury in September and October.[7]

Charles Nodier, however, was most influential in consolidating his younger friend's interest in the Middle Ages, and after trips with Nodier to the coronation of Charles X at Reims and to the Alps, Hugo's observation of both architecture and nature was more profound. A mode of vision in which "la fantaisie prend l'habitude d'accompagner l'observation et fait bon ménage avec elle" began characterizing Hugo's letters and voyage notes.[8] As a result of exposure to Nodier, Hugo's poetry became "jeu de l'imagination, des rythmes et du langage."[9]

No profound changes are evident in three odes, "Aux Ruines de Montfort-l'Amaury," "Le Voyage," and "Promenade," which were inspired by the stay at Montfort-l'Amaury. There is a more accurate observation of architectural detail, but the language and form are conventional.

> Là quelquefois j'entends le luth doux et sévère
> D'un ami qui sait rendre aux vieux temps un trouvère.
> Nous parlons des héros, du ciel, des chevaliers,
> De ces âmes en deuil dans le monde orphelines;
> Et le vent qui se brise à l'angle des ruines
> Gémit dans les hauts peupliers![10]

Hugo's letters indicate something quite different. From Reims he wrote to Adèle that he had slept at Braine, "jolie ville bien bâtie, qui a une autre église en ruines aussi belle que l'abbaye de Jumièges, dont tu as vu les dessins dans le Voyage pittoresque de Nodier."[11] Since Abel Hugo published a study on the Abbey of Saint-Denis in 1825, his brother's enthusiasm for the well-known abbey at Jumièges is not surprising. However, from Hugo's description to his wife of the gothic cathedral at Reims, full of enthusiasm and detail when compared with these remarks about the romanesque church at Jumièges, it is apparent that Nodier had initiated him into the gothic revival.[12]

> J'ai donc été hier visiter la cathédrale. Elle est admirable comme monument d'architecture gothique. Les portails, la rosace, les tours ont un effet particulier. . . . L'intérieur, tel qu'on l'a fait, est beaucoup moins beau qu'il n'était dans sa nudité séculaire. On a peint ce vieux granit en bleu, on a chargé ces sculptures sévères d'or et de clinquant. . . . L'ensemble est satisfaisant pour l'oeil, et il faut avoir médité sur la disposition de l'édifice pour juger qu'on n'en a pas tiré tout le parti possible. Telle qu'elle est, cette décoration annonce encore le progrès des idées romantiques. Il y a six mois, on eût fait un temple grec de la vieille église des Francs.[13]

Hugo's use of accurate architectural vocabulary, his attention to the details of restoration, and his belief that there was a connection between Romanticism and the interest in gothic architecture illustrate how he had become infected by the "contagion d'architecture."[14] By the time he reached the Alps, he was linking the worlds of art and nature and depicting the gothic style as flamboyant and rich in detail. Two peaks are envisaged as having "l'aspect de ces magnifiques cathédrales du moyen-âge, toutes chargées de tours et de tourelles, de lanternes, d'aiguilles, de flèches, de clochers et de clochetons."[15]

A comparison of the prefaces of 1824 and 1826 to the *Odes et Ballades* indicates to what extent Hugo became aware of the Romantic debate in periodicals such as the *Globe* and *Drapeau blanc* and how he came to understand the implications of the Romantic movement for art.[16] In the first preface, Hugo claims he does not know the meanings of the terms "classic" and "romantic"; he cites Madame de Staël's comparison between pagan and Christian literature to explain the distinction. He concludes that there are as many different literatures as there are societies. "En littérature, comme en toute chose, il n'y a que le bon et le mauvais, le beau et le difforme, le vrai et le faux."[17] The poet's function is to march before the people like a light, showing them the path toward the principles of order, morality, and honor in an age of sophism.

Although in the 1826 preface Hugo again refuses to be drawn into the controversy over what constitutes classic and Romantic literature, his position sounds very much like that enunciated by August Wilhelm

Schlegel in his Vienna lectures on dramatic art and literature, suggesting that Hugo had by this time either read the French translation of Schlegel or absorbed his ideas through an intermediary such as the Baron von Eckstein.[18] Hugo has now adopted the Romantic aesthetic of organic unity and the analogy between the gothic cathedral with its seeming irregularity and a literature with a new principle of order. If the creative genius is free, he will create works of true order as opposed to works that exhibit a mere regularity of outer form. Hugo also sees freedom in politics as directly related to freedom in literature. He states this idea indirectly: "Ce qu'il est très important de fixer, c'est qu'en littérature comme en politique l'ordre se concilie merveilleusement avec la liberté; il en est même le résultat."[19] Hugo illustrates "order" with reference to gothic architecture. "Une cathédrale gothique présente un ordre admirable dans sa naïve irrégularité; nos édifices français modernes, auxquels on a si gauchement appliqué l'architecture grecque ou romaine, n'offrent qu'un désordre régulier."[20]

The medieval motifs of the *Ballades* seem strangely at odds with Hugo's observations in his letters, notes, and prefaces, but critics who have considered the medieval elements of the poems have concluded that they are totally conventional. "The medieval element of the *Odes et Ballades*, indeed, is nothing more or less than a smattering of local color: a few descriptions of Gothic churches, castles or ruins, a few references to troubadours, or châtelains or tournaments."[21] "Les pièces sont peu déterminées comme odes, romances ou ballades, mais elles sont bien genre troubadour."[22] Again, the preface of 1826 indicates how Hugo conceived of the form of the *Ballades* and that his aim was to penetrate more deeply into the Middle Ages than had the mediocre writers of the genre troubadour preceding him. Hugo contrasts the poetry of the *Odes* in which he fulfills his social and prophetic functions as poet with that of the *Ballades*. The *Odes* include "toute inspiration purement religieuse, toute étude purement antique, toute traduction d'un événement contemporain ou d'une impression personnelle." The *Ballades* are sketches "d'un genre capricieux: tableaux, rêves, scènes, récits, légendes superstitieuses, traditions populaires." He has tried to give an idea of what the poems of the first troubadours might have been and has therefore put more of his imagination into the *Ballades* and more of his soul into the *Odes*.[23]

Throughout his career, Hugo used the notion of the "poète du caprice" (a poet such as Pindar or Horace) to describe the creator of a poetry of formal elegance and experimentation, a poetry that delights through pure form.[24] As the troubadours "paid for hospitality with songs," entertaining their hosts, Hugo will entertain his nineteenth-century audience with his poems of caprice, creating an equivalent for the authentic medieval poems. In a sense, his *Ballades* mark the culmination of the troubadour tradition which was soon to disappear; Hugo creates a striking form for all the current pseudo-medieval motifs, and having accomplished this, he could then turn his attention to the Orient and write another kind of poetry of caprice in *Les Orientales*.

Hugo did not again publish narrative poetry based on medieval themes until *La Légende des Siècles* in which his political opinions usually color his portrayal of the Middle Ages. Here, since the poetry exists solely as a *jeu*, he does not use the Middle Ages as a vehicle to speak to his own century. The treatment of narration and dramatic situation in the *Ballades* is a prelude to the later "petites épopées," for the medieval portions of the *Légende* provide the occasion for an interesting study of Hugo's relative success in handling narrative poetry in different ways, according to the source of inspiration for each poem. The *ballades* of 1825, which are certainly inspired by the genre troubadour but owe their inspiration as well to German romantic poetry,[25] present either a dramatic situation (the *tableaux, rêves, scènes*) or a narrative (the *récits, légendes, traditions*). The language remains generalized and denotative so that there is little chance for image to become symbol. Paul Zumthor has contrasted the *Ballades* and the medieval poems of *La Légende des Siècles* in terms of imagery, concluding that the earlier images are totally decorative. A specific rhetoric is constituted in which the medieval image is "detached." "En dépit des ténèbres 'funestes' et des voix 'sépulcrales,' nous sommes là, dans un univers linguistiquement rassurant."[26]

"Les Deux Archers" is the first of the group of innovative *ballades* to be written after Hugo's trips to Blois and to Reims.[27] From Nodier Hugo had learned to look for the legend behind the ruins of medieval architecture, and now he links the two in his poetry. Later in *Le Rhin* the decayed monument becomes a symbol of the legend like, for example, the tower of Hatto. The "tour isolée" of "Les Deux Archers" simply provides a vague setting and décor for the legend of the two bowmen who, by their blasphemy, become the prey of the devil. Hugo describes the tower at the beginning of the poem; however, he does indicate that there is a legend behind the tower. When the kings of France were going to the Crusades, the tower was built in three nights "Par un ermite saint qui remuait les pierres/ Avec le signe de la croix" (p. 516). The archers, "sans craindre l'heure," light a fire and seat themselves on the grave of a saint. "Cependant sur la tour, les monts, les bois antiques,/ L'ardent foyer jetait des clartés fantastiques" (p. 516). Hugo uses lighting to heighten the gothic atmosphere, but again the attributive *fantastiques* is no more specific than the terms *isolée, antiques,* and *vieux* which are applied to the architecture.

The same type of setting, "ce paysage sinistre," is provided in *Le Rhin* for the tower of Hatto, the Maüsethurm [*sic*], which Hugo visits. Under the power of the observer's imaginative vision, however, the whole atmosphere in the later description is one of animation, as though the ruins have taken on a sinister life because of the legend of the wicked Hatto which Hugo recounts. Optimum use is made of lighting, sound, and suggestive imagery in this passage.

> A mes pieds, le Rhin courant et se hâtant dans les broussailles avec un murmure rauque et furieux, comme s'il échappait d'un mauvais pas; à droite et à gauche, des montagnes ou plutôt de grosses masses perdant leur sommet dans les nuées d'un ciel sombre piqué çà et là de quelques ètoiles; au fond, pour horizon, un immense rideau d'ombre; au milieu du fleuve, au loin, debout dans une eau plate, huileuse et comme morte, une grande tour noire, d'une forme horrible, du faîte de laquelle sortait, en s'agitant avec des balancements étranges, je ne sais quelle nébulosité rougeâtre.[28]

The fact that the tower of the "Deux Archers" assumes few additional associations in the course of the poem means that the linear progression of the narration is not enhanced by any accumulation of symbolic meanings. Hugo does, however, use the element of lighting to indicate the supernatural forces at work. He thus employs a series of several more specific phrases to explain "clartés fantastiques": "Lueur rampante en bleuâtres sillons," "rayon sulfureux," "flamme bleuâtre," and "flamme infernale." The extinguishing of these lights eventually marks the end of Satanic power and the climax of the narrative movement: "Alors tout s'éteignit, flammes, rires, phosphore" (p. 518). In this way Hugo objectifies the movement of the *récit* in the visual effects of the poem.

The verse structure (a six-line stanza of five alexandrines and a final octosyllable in an aabccb pattern), though lending itself to a fast-moving narration, is not used for special effects. Instead, Hugo divides the poem into two halves; after the initial "incident," he repeats, with some variation, the fourth stanza of the poem, thus introducing the second "incident," the breaking of the Satanic spell. The atmosphere of the legend dissipates in the final stanza when Hugo moralizes and draws the parallel between the blasphemy of the two archers and the unbelief of his own century. "Nul, dans notre âge aveugle et vain de ses sciences,/ Ne sait plier les deux genoux!" (p. 518).

"La Ronde du sabbat," written in October of 1825, is a tableau which again depicts the twilight world of the supernatural. The vocabulary is still picturesque: "ce noir monastère," "clartés," "rayons bleus," "rouges flammes," "toits rompus," and "portails brisés." Nevertheless, the handling of time is quite different from that of "Les Deux Archers," which was a narrative legend. The introductory alexandrines by their dramatic direct address, rhetorical questions, and exclamations set the stage for the coming *ronde*. As the witches' dance begins, a spell also is created that is broken in the last stanza when we realize suddenly that time has passed. "L'aube pâle a blanchi les arches colossales./ Il fuit, l'essaim confus des démons dispersés!"(p. 545). The actual movement of the dance, recreated in the six-syllable, nine-line stanzas and in the two-line refrain of the central portion of the ballad, thus replaces the linear progression of time through narrative sequence.

As the *ronde* gets under way, Hugo drops the rhetorical tone characterizing the initial lines and quickens the pace of the poetry as he describes the Satanic participants. "Soudain la ronde/ Comme un ouragan sombre, en tournoyant commence" (p. 542). The chants of the dancers convey a sabbat having no roots in a historical medieval past, but in the long-existing craze for the occult — evident in Goethe, Cazotte, and Nodier. Perhaps the interest is typified by the *Dictionnaire infernal* of Collin de Plancy which Hugo knew at least by the time he wrote *Notre-Dame de Paris*.

> Satan vous verra!
> De vos mains grossières,
> Parmi des poussières,
> Ecrivez, sorcières:
> ABRACADABRA!
>
> (P. 544)[29]

A similar verse structure is used in "La Mêlée" (September 1825), but with variation in the narration. This *ballade* treats quite another tradition than "Les Deux Archers" and "La Ronde du sabbat"; this was epic action as it was supposed by the Romantics to exist in the *chanson de geste*. The poem is a narrative placed in the dramatic frame of an account of the action given to an onlooking shepherd who is addressed in the first and final stanzas. Hugo imports the pastoral element into the epic action. Yet the narration of the combat between the Normans and the Celts does not proceed to a conclusion without interruption. Hugo uses six-line stanzas of alexandrines to recount the combat, and he intersperses these with octosyllabic stanzas of ten lines each in imitation of the action of the battle. Hugo again solves the problem of bringing the action to a close and indicating the passing of time by the convention of the coming of night. "Viens, berger: la nuit tombe, et plus de sang ruisselle"; "Viens, laissons achever cette lutte brûlante" (p. 515). This *ballade* has little of the atmosphere of the picturesque, but the vocabulary remains "decorative." Hugo lists a series of terms, giving the illusion of action, and this catalogue replaces the detailed narration of individual combat in the *chanson de geste:* "Dagues, halle-bardes, épées,/ Pertuisanes de sang trempées,/ Haches, poignards à deux tranchants" (p. 514).[30]

Both "Écoute-moi, Madeleine" and "la Fiancée du timbalier" follow closely the ballad tradition as it came to France from England and Germany. The second poem is interesting because, unlike Bürger's "Lénore," which Hugo knew in translation, the legend is not recounted by a third-person narrator. Instead, a dramatic monologue becomes the vehicle for the narration, and as the account of events progresses from the past to the description of the parade by of the returning soldiers in the present, the reader becomes increasingly aware of the discrepancy between the hope of the fiancée to see her returning drummer and the actual possibility of his return. In the final stanza, as the fiancée dies, there is an abrupt shift from the dramatic monologue to an objective narration; the effect is theatrical, but it intensifies the preceding irony.

The three *ballades* written in 1828 reflect Hugo's increasing fascina-tion for experimenting with verse forms as part of the new Romantic aesthetic, and provide variations of the medieval motifs used in 1825. "La Chasse du burgrave," for example, is again written as a dramatic-narrative, but this time the tone seems to be ironic. The playful verse form matches this tone with which Hugo handles the theme of the *senex* who is cuckolded while he is away hunting. "On t'a vengé. — Fille d'Autriche/ Triche/ Quand l'hymen lui donne un barbon/ Bon." (p. 527).

"Le Pas d'armes du roi Jean," focuses on chivalrous combat, but by no means on the combat of a *chanson de geste.* The three-syllable lines are used in a kind of telegraphic style which results in a fast-moving series of scenes rather than in a full-blown narration. The focal point of these scenes is Paris: "Cette ville,/ Aux longs cris,/ Qui profile/ Son front gris,/ Des toits frêles,/ Cent tourelles,/ Clochers grêles,/ C'est Paris!" (pp. 529–30). But this seems to be the Paris of François Ier because Hugo refers to a highly conventionalized society and such sixteenth-century figures as Gaspard de Saulx-Tavane and Guy Chabat.

This tendency to couple the sixteenth century with the Middle Ages is a curious aspect of the Romantic desire to learn about the past. Of course, in 1828 Hugo was influenced by Sainte-Beuve, who published his *Tableau historique et critique de la poésie française et du théâtre français au XVIe siècle* in that year. Since the Pléiade poets were models for a new literature, it was natural for Hugo to lump together under the category of "vieux poètes" both the troubadours and later writers such as Ron-sard and Du Bellay. The various epigraphs from the renaissance poets

Hugo added to the *Ballades* in 1828 illustrate how his interests were turning away from the genre troubadour itself. However, in making few distinctions between medieval and renaissance poetry, Hugo was probably following the example of Nodier, who had done the same thing as early as 1818.[31]

"La Légende de la nonne" is written in the tradition of gothic horror tales, most notably Lewis's *The Monk*. As in "Les Deux Archers," Hugo's two-part narrative consists of an initial incident, the nun's loss of virtue as she falls into the power of Satan, and of the legend of the wanderings of the nun's ghost. A quality reflecting the oral origins of a Spanish romance is given the narration by the opening lines: "Venez, vous dont l'oeil étincelle,/ Pour entendre une histoire encor,/ Approchez: je vous dirai celle/ De doña Padilla del Flor" (p. 535).

This seems to be the first time that Hugo brings the medieval architectural imagery to life and, in turn, animates the legend. A "cloître gothique" (a *topos* in the conventions of the medieval vogue Hugo used in his early poetry) is now transformed in appearance during the night hours.

> Quand la nuit, du cloître gothique
> Brunissant les portails béants,
> Change à l'horizon fantastique
> Les deux clochers en deux géants. . . .

> (P. 538)

The ghosts of the nun and the brigand whom she loved are doomed to wander in an eternal search for one another, for they find themselves on illusionary staircases. "Mais ce sont des escaliers fées,/ Qui sous eux s'embrouillent toujours." The context of the image of the "magiques spirales" differs from the *merveilleux* of the earlier *Odes*. The "escaliers fées" probably reflect Hugo's early, indirect acquaintance with Piranesi but, in any case, mark the assimilation of "the spiral, the labyrinth and the interior of Babel" into Hugo's imaginative vision.[32] Because of the gradual evolution of Hugo's use of architectural imagery in connection with narration, the "Légende de la nonne" becomes a steppingstone to the novel technique of *Notre-Dame de Paris*. Architecture takes on life, assumes a symbolic significance within a narrative pattern, and conjures up the darker side of existence. Subtly, the fantastic elements he perceived in the Middle Ages dominated Hugo's interpretation of the period, taking on a new significance in his literary creation.

La Préface de Cromwell reveals how Hugo had assimilated the Middle Ages into his maturing imaginative vision, for he illustrates his theory of the grotesque with examples drawn from medieval culture.[33] A series of phrases jotted in the manuscript of the *Odes et Ballades* illustrates how Hugo's mind connected history, medieval architecture, and the grotesque. The order of the phrases is: "Ceci je sais sur l'histoire universelle" — "du grotesque" — "de l'architecture du moyen âge." Four sketches of different types of pediments and columns follow with the subtitles "égyptienne," "grecque," "romaine," and "romane."[34] These phrases and sketches could, in effect, serve as a résumé of the *Préface*.

For the first time in his own statements on literary theory, Hugo associates Christianity with the modern (Romantic) era of poetry, echoing Madame de Staël, among others. The Middle Ages thus ushered in the modern era of literature, broadening the scope of art and permitting the genre of drama to develop. The modern muse "sentira que tout dans la création n'est pas humainement *beau,* que le laid y existe à côté du beau, le difforme près du gracieux, le grotesque au revers du sublime, le mal avec le bien, l'ombre avec la lumière."[35]

Hugo's discussion of the Middle Ages as a Christian era, especially in connection with the grotesque, is ambivalent. It has been noted that the *Génie du christianisme* did not lead Hugo to portray the medieval period as Christian in his poetry, and though the preface to the *Odes* of 1823 promises to replace pagan mythology with a Christian theogony, the *Ballades* reveal more of the supernatural and fantastic than of a Christian theogony. Hugo's imaginative vision and new literary aesthetic overshadowed his own rather tenuous religious orthodoxy at this time; he is fascinated by the superstitions of the Middle Ages. A result of the grotesque is that it "attache autour de la religion mille superstitions originales" (p. 199). Much of the *Préface* has nothing to do with the Middle Ages, but the references to medieval art are characterized in Hugo's mind by a grotesque quality. In fact, the medieval mentality is an extension of his own interests; the grotesque becomes a creative force, like "la chimère gothique" described later in *Promontorium somnii.* "C'est lui [le grotesque] qui sème à pleines mains dans l'air, dans l'eau, dans la terre, dans le feu, ces myriades d'êtres intermédiaires que nous retrouvons tout vivants dans les traditions populaires du moyen âge. . . . C'est lui, toujours lui, qui tantôt jette dans l'enfer chrétien ces hideuses figures qu'évoquera l'âpre génie de Dante" (pp. 199–200). The grotesque, suggesting the dark side of the Middle Ages through ritual and superstition, for the first time symbolizes the people.

In the preface to the *Odes et Ballades* of 1826, Hugo had stressed the organic order behind the irregularity of the gothic cathedral; *La Préface de Cromwell* indicates that the source of this irregularity lies in the grotesque. Hugo's notion of the grotesque sometimes borders on being synonymous with "the ugly" and elsewhere seems to suggest a juxtaposition of contrasting individual elements within a larger aesthetic context, but it would seem to be an extension of the Romantic desire to enlarge the confines of aesthetic beauty and unity.[36] The grotesque stamps its character on the preeminent art form of the Middle Ages. "Il attache son stigmate au front des cathédrales, encadre ses enfers et ses purgatoires sous l'ogive des portails, les fait flamboyer sur les vitraux, déroule ses monstres, ses dogues, ses démons autour des chapiteaux, le long des frises, au bord du toit" (pp. 209–10). The grotesque transforms all gothic architecture into one flamboyant style and suggests that the image of the late gothic was fixed in Hugo's mind.

In the *Préface* Dante is a great writer who used the grotesque to enhance the beauty of his work. "Croit-on que Françoise de Rimini et Béatrix seraient aussi ravissantes chez un poète qui ne nous enfermerait pas dans la tour de la Faim et ne nous forcerait point à partager le repoussant repas d'Ugolin? Dante n'aurait pas tant de grâce, s'il n'avait pas tant de force" (pp. 203–4). To the Romantics, Dante was synonymous with the poet's exile from society; Rivarol emphasizes this view in the introduction to his translation of the Inferno.[37] He also underscores Dante's vision of Hell as a spiral;[38] since Hugo's interest in that image developed at this time, he may have read Rivarol's translation. Hugo probably knew only the *Inferno,* but he is the first of the Romantics to incorporate Dante's ideas into the new aesthetic. Chateaubriand, for example, reprinted Rivarol's translation of the Paolo and Francesca passage, but considered the *Comedy* a bizarre production whose beauties came from Christianity and whose faults derived from the taste of the poet and his age. Even Madame de Staël, in her novel *Corinne,* spoke only of the "enchaînement mystique de cercles et de sphères" and of the "mythologie de l'imagination" which were evident in the *Inferno.*[39] Hugo repeats the association of Dante and the grotesque in 1830, coupling Dante with Rabelais and juxtaposing the late Middle Ages and sixteenth century once again. "Et la nature, au fond des siècles et des nuits,/ Accouplant Rabelais à Dante plein d'ennuis/ Et l'Ugolin sinistre au Grandgousier difforme,/ Près de l'immense deuil montre le rire énorme."[40] Several of the poems of the *Orientales,* published early in 1829, also illustrate Hugo's growing interest in Dante, for they are preceded by epigraphs from the *Inferno.*[41]

Although Hugo had not begun to associate himself with Dante, the visionary and political exile, he assimilated those aspects of the *Inferno* that accorded with his own taste and reinforced other pictorial images he had absorbed. At almost the same time that he discovered Dante, Hugo became aware of Dürer, the other major medieval artist with whom he would identify. "Un Dessin d'Albert Dürer" dates from December 1827 and shares the same verse form as "La Chasse du burgrave," written the next month. The *ballade* includes a description of a somber landscape at midnight, an enumeration of the gathering of the ghosts of the dead, and the poet's meditation on the theme of death. Hugo uses a decorative vocabulary to describe the scene, afterwards creating a clever rhyme based on essential elements of conventional poetic language: "la mer sombre," "le manoir noir," "la tour inhospitalière," "le haut donjon," "les colossales salles," "la cloche . . . tint," "la tombe," "les ombres sombres." Hugo does not seem to have a particular work by Dürer in mind, but he links him with the supernatural, the picturesque, and the theme of death. "Ains la mort nous chasse et nous foule,/ Foule/ De héros petits et d'étroits/ Rois."[42]

Les Orientales is part of the "renaissance orientale," that revival of the exotic which paralleled the medieval craze. Hugo's preface to these poems includes even stronger statements of the need for aesthetic unity through rich variety than the theoretical statements of the 1820s. No doubt his increasing consciousness of color, detail, and formal experimentation was a direct result of his contacts with artists such as Boulanger, Delacroix, the Devéria brothers, the architect and enthusiast for the gothic — Charles Robelin, and Sainte-Beuve in the *cénacle* which met on the rue Notre-Dame-des-Champs during 1827 and 1828. Calling this volume a "livre inutile de pure poésie" — a poetry like that of the *Ballades* — Hugo enlarges the subject matter of French poetry in general. He therefore defends both the Orient and the Middle Ages. "Là [dans l'Orient], en effet, tout est grand, riche, fécond, comme dans le moyen-âge, cette autre mer de poésie. . . . Jusqu'ici on a beaucoup trop vu l'époque moderne dans le siècle de Louis XIV, et l'antiquité dans Rome et la Grèce; ne verrait-on pas de plus haut et plus loin, en étudiant l'ère moderne dans le moyen-âge et l'antiquité dans l'Orient?"[43] To illustrate further his ideas, Hugo paints a picture of a medieval Spanish village in all its dazzling variety with the gothic cathedral situated at one end and the mosque at the other; he covets for France a literature as rich in complexity as that medieval village. His description of the flamboyant gothic with its explosion of detail conveys variety in an overall unity and includes the analogy between the pillars of the cathedral and a forest which had been introduced into France by Chateaubriand.

> . . . la grande cathédrale gothique avec ses hautes flèches tailladées en scies, sa large tour du bourdon, ses cinq portails brodés de bas-reliefs, sa frise à jour comme une collerette, ses solides arcs-boutants si frêles à l'oeil; et puis, ses cavités profondes, sa forêt de piliers à chapiteaux bizarres; . . . merveilleux édifice, imposant par sa masse, curieux par ses détails, beau à deux lieues et beau à deux pas. (P. 579)

In *Les Orientales* a few poems such as "La Bataille perdue" and "Le

Château-fort" treat familiar themes first used in the *Odes*. Two other poems from 1828 are of interest, for they relate to the *ballades* of the same period. "Romance mauresque" was inspired directly by one of Abel's translations, "Mort de Don Rodrigue de Lara." Hugo again uses a short stanza and line to give the poem an "oral" quality; this verse form reinforces the narration and dialogue by which the poem proceeds. The picturesque is noticeably absent from the meeting of the unarmed Don Rodrigue and his nephew Mudarra, whom he has been chasing to avenge the deaths of the seven sons of Lara. As in "La Fiancée du timbalier," irony concludes the progression within the poem. In this case, the irony is cruel as the Moor Mudarra shows no mercy toward his uncle, proclaiming that he will kill Rodrigue with the very sword which symbolizes the honor of the family. To the end Rodrigue mistakenly expects a semblance of honor from Mudarra, whom Hugo almost caricatures as the pagan Moor, but the former is killed as he awaits permission to arm.

As Pierre Albouy has noted, the spirit of "Les Djinns," with its oncoming army of vampires, seems closer to the "Ronde du sabbat" than to the Orient.[44] Hugo attempts to recreate movement by his stanza pattern just as he does in the *ballade*. In the first case there is a stanza of fixed length; here there is a pattern of stanzas of varying lengths as the swarm of the *Djinns* passes. The progression depends entirely upon this somewhat restrictive device and upon the dramatic quality of the poet's reactions to the creatures. To a certain extent, Hugo uses onomatopoeia to imitate the sound of the oncoming *Djinns*, but the focus of the poem is more on its structure and on the rhetoric of the poet's reactions.

> Dieu! la voix sépulcrale
> Des Djinns! . . . Quel bruit ils font!
> Fuyons sous la spirale
> De l'escalier profond.

(P. 654)

Except for this passage, the picturesque décor of the *Ballades* is almost absent. Here, however, the spiral staircase, which appeared in "La Légende de la nonne," takes on an obvious psychological force which suggests the narrator's own fear. The transformation of a visual detail into a symbolic force marks the beginning of the disappearance of the picturesque per se from Hugo's poetic creation.

By 1828, Hugo had already begun to think about *Notre-Dame de Paris*.[45] He was also writing *Le Dernier Jour d'un condamné*, a unique psychological study. In chapter 36, the condemned man recalls his childhood visit to the bell tower of the Notre-Dame cathedral. Several elements of Hugo's later portrayal of the cathedral are already here in embryo form: "le sombre escalier en colimaçon," "la place du Parvis Notre-Dame," the "étourdissement" caused by the ringing of the bell. Again, concentration on visual details of medieval architecture is a part of a tendency to give symbolic value to the concrete.

Also significant in the evolution of Hugo's medievalism is the irony with which he treats the troubadour craze in the preface to the third edition of the novel, "Une Comédie à propos d'une tragédie" (1829). This preface clarifies Hugo's opposition to capital punishment, but the point is made indirectly. Psychological realism is contrasted with the prevailing artificial literary taste. An elegiac poet reads some verses to a salon — verses straight from the troubadour tradition. When he is criticized for being Romantic, and not employing the term *gothique* instead of *antique,* the poet defends himself by saying that he is Romantic, "mais modéré." He then turns attention from himself by mentioning *Le Dernier Jour d'un condamné.* In the discussion which follows, Hugo mocks the horror that his attack on capital punishment has aroused, and in doing so, he places himself in a camp opposite that of the troubadour sentimentalists.

The years 1828 and 1829 are important in measuring the intensity of Hugo's interest in the Middle Ages. He paid his dues to the *topoi* of the genre troubadour, and he absorbed ideas from medieval culture: the symbolic figure of Dante and the gothic cathedral became constants to be used again and again. Hugo's affinity for the flamboyant gothic and for the grotesque illustrates his progression beyond Chateaubriand and an assimilation of medieval culture corresponding to the new Romantic aesthetic. Emphasis on the fantastic, on the dark side of the popular mind, corresponds to Hugo's own impulses as a visionary, but also to the interpretation of the late Middle Ages which was important in France at the time. As a result, medieval history, the "waning" Middle Ages of Louis XI, the period of malaise and of the *danse macabre,* became the focal point of Hugo's attention as he planned *Notre-Dame de Paris.*

4

Notre-Dame de Paris

Politics, Progress, and the Middle Ages

Notre-Dame de Paris represents Hugo's first attempt to capture and recreate the spirit and color of the late Middle Ages; as such, the novel also ends the initial period of his medievalism. Hugo had to interrupt the writing of the book during 1830 because of the July Revolution, and the work is marked by his emerging consciousness of historical and political movement. *La Préface de Cromwell* had already indicated an awareness of Romantic views originating in Germany and of historical change and progress by indicating a correspondence between three ages of civilization and three literary genres — the ode, the epic, and the drama.[1] "Le genre humain dans son ensemble a grandi, s'est développé, a mûri comme un de nous. Il a été enfant, il a été homme; nous assistons maintenant à son imposante vieillesse."[2] In describing the nature of modern drama, Hugo had revealed a further detail of his deepened interest in history by forcefully stating that "local color" must permeate the work. "Le drame doit être radicalement imprégné de cette couleur des temps; elle doit en quelque sorte y être dans l'air, de façon qu'on ne s'aperçoive qu'en y entrant et qu'en en sortant qu'on a changé de siècle et de l'atmosphère."[3] Hugo's use of the novel form and of the fifteenth century in *Notre-Dame de Paris* constitutes an extension of these ideas enunciated in 1827.

In choosing to portray the late Middle Ages, Hugo followed a number of other writers, all of whom had depicted a period of social change and unrest — a rather negative tableau of the waning of a civilization. By 1840 Barante's *Histoire des Ducs de Bourgogne* and *Notre-Dame de Paris* itself were responsible for a certain view of late medieval France. "The picture called up by these would have been grim and dark, scarcely illuminated by any ray of serenity and beauty."[4] The reason for this rather bleak view of the period lies in the fact that the Romantics derived their information chiefly from the medieval chronicles.

Barante's preface to his history clarifies the prevailing nineteenth-century attitudes toward history writing and the interpretation of fifteenth-century France which Hugo would have shared. The narrators of history in France, according to Barante, have always shared certain characteristics: "juger et raconter à la fois; manifester tous les dons de l'imagination dans la peinture exacte de la vérité; se plaire à tout ce qui a de la vie et du mouvement; laisser au lecteur, comme à soi-même, son libre arbitre pour blâmer et approuver; allier une sorte de douce ironie à une impartiale bienveillance."[5] Interpreters of history have forgotten the importance of narration because the elements that give life to history have disappeared from their annals. As a result, fictional characters often seem more alive than actual historical characters, and Barante concludes that the historian must take pleasure in "painting" more than in "analyzing." He should also take pains not to introduce his own conceptions into the events of the past, creating "une sorte de costume théâtral."[6] Since in antiquity history was a branch of literature, nineteenth-century historians should be encouraged by the new interest in the past. Barante wants to restore the prestige history had lost with the rise of the historical novel. The events he is describing have a particular appeal to contemporaneous readers because of the power of the people in the later Middle Ages, and he has tried to recreate the vitality of those events through quotations and speeches drawn from sources of the time. "On demeure convaincu, avec une sorte de satisfaction, que même dans ces temps barbares où régnait la force, . . . la pensée et la voix du peuple exerçaient déjà un immense pouvoir. On remarque comment la plus extrême violence éprouvait le besoin de se faire autoriser de l'approbation publique, et la recherchait par l'hypocrisie et le mensonge."[7]   **1919338**

This tableau of fifteenth-century society conveys the idea of a civilization based on power, force, and the distinction between the barbarous victor and the vanquished who are degraded in defeat. The brief reign of Charles V corresponds to the rise of the people creating "une démocratie turbulente et barbare, toujours prête aux plus sanglantes séditions, ennemie impitoyable de la noblesse et de la chevalerie, qui semblait la cause de tous ces maux."[8] Barante concludes by expressing the hope that if, as a result of this history, his readers are able to discern among all peoples an order and well-being in present-day civilization which did not exist at the time of their oppressed ancestors, he will have accomplished a useful task.

Barante's preface indicates just how great the appeal of the color, vitality, and change of the late Middle Ages was for the nineteenth century, but it is clearly an age of oppression in which popular movement prefigures later social progress. His point of view aligns him with Romanticism and liberalism. Walter Scott, who was also attracted to periods of historical flux and change, used the chronicles in writing *Quentin Durward,* relying heavily on the *Mémoires* of Commines and the *Chronique scandaleuse* of Jean de Roye. The popularity of *Quentin*

Durward in France both contributed to and coincided with the interest in the courts of Charles the Bold and Louis XI, especially as described by Commines.[9] Scott saw the throne of France threatened by potential anarchy and was therefore unsympathetic to popular uprisings; yet he understood that the end of the feudal order was inevitable. He chose to embody the conflicts of the end of the Middle Ages in Louis XI. "At this time," Scott writes, "and as if to save their fair realm from the various woes with which it was menaced, the tottering throne was ascended by Louis XI, whose character, evil as it was in itself, met, combated, and in a great degree neutralised the mischiefs of the time."[10] The events of the novel, principally the disastrous interview with Charles the Bold at Péronne in 1468 when Louis was held under house arrest while Liège was in a turmoil instigated by the French king, bear out Scott's opinions of Louis, and the novelist popularized in France this somewhat warped picture of the French king.

Mérimée's historical drama, *La Jaquerie* (1828), is also based on the medieval chronicles, this time those of Froissart. A "chronicle play" in prose, it is subtitled "Scènes féodales" and its "diffuse" structure reflects Mérimée's use of Shakespeare as a model.[11] In choosing the peasant revolt of the fourteenth century as his subject, Mérimée evidently wanted to qualify the opinions of Froissart, who was biased in favor of the aristocrasy. "Une révolte de paysans semble inspirer un profond dégoût à cet historien, qui se complaît à célébrer les beaux coups de lance et les prouesses de nobles chevaliers. Quant aux causes qui produisirent la Jaquerie, il n'est pas difficile de les deviner. Les excès de la féodalité durent amener d'autres excès."[12] Mérimée also justifies his choice of a priest (Frère Jean) to lead the revolt as "vraisemblable" because John Ball had helped instigate Wat Tyler's revolt of 1381 in England. He defends his use of imaginative detail to fill in the lacunae of the chronicles. "J'ai tâché de donner une idée des moeurs atroces du XIVe siècle, et je crois avoir plutôt adouci que rembruni les couleurs de mon tableau."[13] Mérimée thus idealizes the early stage of the revolt, indicates the peasants' betrayal by the English, and paints an aristocracy in decline. Gilbert d'Apremont, against whom Loup-garou (the violent peasant leader) and Frère Jean are seeking vengeance, declares early in the play that "les vieilles coutumes se perdent, et avec elles aussi les vertus de nos ancêtres."[14]

When *La Jaquerie* was reviewed by the *Globe,* the critic approved of Mérimée's choice of subject matter. "*La Jaquerie* est un beau sujet, et un sujet difficile. Episode presque isolé dans nos annales, c'est un événement, le seul peut-être, qui a mis en mouvement toutes les classes de la société."[15] Reflecting the liberal view of inevitable social change, the critic discusses the short-lived nature of the revolt and says that the peasants, once put down, were silent until the memorable day when the centuries would give them the right to speak. The reviewer also compares *La Jaquerie* with Goethe's *Götz von Berlichingen,* noting that there is no character of the grandeur of Götz in Mérimée's play. "Après tout, la pièce de Goethe est le premier essai, le premier exemple de ce retour au moyen âge par l'imagination, de ce goût pour les peintures gothiques et nationales, qui envahit maintenant tous les arts."[16]

One further example will illustrate the coalescence of interpreta-tions of the waning Middle Ages, the social unrest of the peasantry, the nature of the monarchy, and the decline of feudalism, evident in *Notre-Dame de Paris,* and representative of the time. In 1840, Michelet drew contrasting portraits of Charles VI and Louis XI. First, he saw the oncoming madness of Charles as symbolic of the atmosphere of a strange era. "Ce sont d'étranges époques. On nie, on croit tout. Une fiévreuse atmosphère de superstition sceptique enveloppe les villes sombres. L'ombre augmente dans leurs rues étroites; leur brouillard va s'épaississant aux fumées d'alchimie et de sabbat."[17] Michelet calls the extraordinary fests and the formalism of the court of Burgundy vain symbolism in comparison with the emerging modern mind which he sees represented by Louis XI. "Ce génie inquiet reçut en naissant tous les instincts modernes, bons et mauvais, mais par-dessus tout l'impatience de détruire, le mépris du passé; c'était un esprit vif, sec, prosaïque."[18] Despite long humiliations, the astuteness and patience of Louis enabled him to succeed, but historians have forgotten the methods the king used to gain his ends. "Un autre mal, très-grave, et qui fausse l'histoire, c'est que la féodalité, périssant sous une telle main, eut l'air de périr victime d'un guet-apens. Le dernier de chaque maison resta le *bon* duc, le *bon* comte. La féodalité, ce vieux tyran caduc, gagna fort à mourir de la main d'un tyran."[19]

It was natural for Hugo, who had reviewed *Quentin Durward* for the *Muse française,* to choose the fifteenth century as the historical setting of his novel and to call Louis XI the workman who began the demolition of the feudal edifice. The chroniclers used by Scott — Commines and Jean de Roye — plus the biography of Louis XI by Mathieu also reinforced Hugo's ambivalent feelings about the fifteenth century as an age of oppression but of social change, as well.[20] In addition to these immediate sources and such writers as Barante and Mérimée, Hugo's interpretation of Paris under Louis XI undoubtedly reflects his own changing political stance and the July Revolution. The movement within history is the movement of the *peuple,* unthinking, pitiless, and pious.[21] The ode "A la Colonne de la Place Vendôme" (1827) had marked the beginning of Hugo's political *engagement* and an evolution-ary process by which nationalism and liberalism became linked symbol-ically for a time with Napoleon and Charlemagne.

Further, Hugo came to praise the Revolution of 1789 and the rise of the people as inevitable until in 1834, in his essay "Sur Mirabeau," he would conclude that the Revolution had opened an immense book, "une sorte de grand testament" for all social theories. Thus, in Hugo's "liberal" stance of 1830, the goal of historical change was a unified society under strong leadership which would give *le peuple* its just rights. When in *Hernani* Don Carlos cries "Rois! regardez en bas!/ — Ah! le peuple! — océan! — onde sans cesse émue" and is inspired by the example of Charlemagne, the early Middle Ages is a metaphor for the national unity Hugo would like to see in France.[22] But in *Notre-Dame de Paris*, the fifteenth century is a metaphor for a society in change. The analogy between movement of the ocean and the rise of the masses within history is pervasive at this time, indicating just how strong Hugo's historical consciousness had become.

> Ecoutez! écoutez, à l'horizon immense,
> Ce bruit qui parfois tombe et soudain recommence,
> Ce murmure confus, ce sourd frémissement
> Qui roule, et qui s'accroît de moment en moment.
> C'est le peuple qui vient, c'est la haute marée
> Qui monte incessamment, par son astre attirée.[23]

The new literature of the Romantics was called a "littérature du style symbolique" by Pierre Leroux of *Le Globe*.[24] In this important article, Leroux maintains that all poetry is metaphoric and that the poet is an artist "qui saisit des rapports de tout genre par toutes les puissances de son âme, et qui leur substitue des rapports identiques sous forme d'images, de même que le géomètre substitue au contraire des termes purement abstraits, des lettres qui ne représentent rien de déterminé, aux nombres, aux lignes, aux surfaces, aux solides, à tous les corps de la nature, et à tous les phénomènes."[25] The symbol is a special kind of metaphor, situated between the simile and allegory: "l'artifice de cette forme de langage consiste à ne pas développer l'idée que l'on veut comparer à une autre, mais à développer uniquement cette seconde idée, c'est-à-dire l'image."[26] Hugo is described as a writer of this symbolic style; in fact, he cannot endure any abstraction in his poetry. After the July Revolution, another article in the *Globe*, written perhaps by Sainte-Beuve, stressed that Romantic literature could no longer be disinterested, that art had to share the passions of the throng or lapse into silence.[27]

With such ideas being discussed in the liberal press, it is hardly surprising that politics colored Hugo's discussion of the masses and medieval architecture in *Notre-Dame de Paris*. Even the followers of Saint-Simon viewed the Middle Ages in terms of their own religious and social theories. Since they preferred order to anarchy, they praised the Middle Ages as the last unified period, but they were not partisans of the past. Only religion could reveal the secret of historical progress, so, to understand the future, it was necessary to study the religions of the past.[28] Something of this double vision exists in Hugo, and certainly his admiration of the unity of the Holy Roman Empire and his disturbance before the disintegration of society in the later Middle Ages parallel Saint-Simonism, but Hugo's orientation in interpreting fifteenth-century Paris is based on political and aesthetic ideas as well as on religious convictions.[29]

Concern for the people as a collective whole causes Hugo to frame the entire novel between two spectacular movements: the "fête des fous" and the attack of the inhabitants of the "Cour des Miracles" on Notre-Dame cathedral. In this sense, the people of Paris become as important for the setting of *Notre-Dame de Paris* as the architecture. In the first chapter, the crowd gathered in the great hall of the Palais de Justice has the "aspect d'une mer" (p. 13); the city of Paris, viewed from the cathedral, becomes "cet amas d'habitations bourgeoises," and the roofs are like "des vagues d'une mer" (p. 152). When the crowd ascends the cathedral to avenge the death of Jehan du Moulin, the brother of Claude Frollo, it is transformed into "cette marée ascendante de faces épouvantables" (p. 483). In interpreting the mentality of the masses, the perspective of Hugo the nineteenth-century novelist is apparent. "Le peuple, au moyen-âge surtout, est dans la société ce qu'est l'enfant dans la famille. Tant qu'il reste dans cet état d'ignorance première, de minorité morale et intellectuelle, on peut dire de lui comme de l'enfant: 'Cet âge est sans pitié' " (p. 268). Speaking of the immured recluse, Hugo notes that "la piété peu raisonneuse et peu subtile de ce temps-là ne voyait pas tant de facettes à un acte de religion. Elle prenait la chose en bloc . . . et s'en apitoyait médiocrement" (p. 239).

This is an age in which the people have not yet attained any degree of power, though the society in Paris is less feudal than bourgeois. Jacques Coppenole, self-made man and member of the Dutch embassy which had come in 1482 to negotiate the marriage of Margaret of Flanders to the Dauphin, appears as a kind of spokesman for the people during both moments of popular force that frame the novel. At the performance of the mystery play during the "fête des fous" when Coppenole is introduced as a *huissier* and corrects the introduction to *chaussetier,* he is cheered by the crowd.[30] A paragraph added later to the manuscript follows which emphasizes the character of the people. "Ajoutons que Coppenole était du peuple, et que ce public qui l'entourait était du peuple. Aussi la communication entre eux et lui avait été prompte, électrique, et pour ainsi dire de plain-pied" (p. 48). After the attack on the cathedral is under way Coppenole assumes a prophetic role; the Dutchman declares that the hour of the people is not yet imminent, but that it is certain to come (pp. 512–13).

The trio of main characters might appear initially to be simply three "types" who reappear constantly within the *oeuvre* of Hugo: the doomed *proscrit*, the monster figure, and idealized feminine beauty. Frollo, Quasimodo, and Esmeralda are not *vraisemblables* when judged according to the canons of realism. Relying on sources such as Collin de Plancy, Du Breul, and Sauval, Hugo surrounds these three characters with an aura of the fantastic. But the Parisians within the novel create a myth for the three figures, and it is clear that popular belief accepted the fantastic as part of the normal course of events. Before he ever tells the history of Quasimodo, for example, Hugo gives the reader this glimpse of the dark side of the medieval imagination as Quasimodo appears at the *fête des fous*.

> Les femmes en effet se cachaient le visage.
> — Oh! le vilain singe, disait l'une.
> — Aussi méchant que laid, reprenait une autre.
> — C'est le diable, ajoutait une troisième. . . .
> — Je suis sûre qu'il va au sabbat. Une fois, il a laissé
> un balai sur mes plombs. (P. 62)

Among the people, Claude Frollo's reputation as a scholar is also transformed by the superstitious mind. "Du cloître, sa réputation de savant avait été au peuple, où elle avait un peu tourné, chose fréquente alors, au renom de sorcier" (p. 175). Phoebus, who is interested in Esmeralda and is stabbed eventually by the priest in a jealous frenzy, is called "indévot et superstitieux." He sees in Esmeralda and her love "beaucoup plus de magie que d'amour, probablement une sorcière, peut-être le diable; une comédie enfin, ou, pour parler le langage d'alors, un mystère très désagréable où il jouait un rôle fort gauche, le rôle des coups et des risées" (pp. 387–88). In these descriptions, Hugo intensifies the element of the grotesque which he first portrayed as an active part of the medieval imagination in *La Préface de Cromwell*, and he underscores the difference between the mature mind of the modern reader and the mental attitudes of the medieval populace.

The pathetic dimension of the people becomes a dominating theme of the novel. Unenlightened humanity suffers, and it glimpses only now and then the possibility of freedom. The two sources of power which cause this suffering are the Church and the Throne. Hugo accentuates the lack of civil justice and the acceptance of this injustice. Both Louis XI and his magistrates are indicted indirectly for the sufferings of Quasimodo and Esmeralda, representatives of the oppressed people. Robert d'Estouteville, provost of Paris, becomes the object of much irony in the chapter entitled "Coup d'oeil impartial sur l'ancienne magistrature." He has literally hung on to his position and become one with it despite the penchant of Louis XI to keep changing his counselors.[31] "C'était donc une très douce et plaisante existence que celle de messire Robert. . . . N'était-ce rien que d'exercer haute et basse justice, droit de tourner, de pendre et de traîner?" (pp. 226, 227). Hugo is much more scathing in his attacks on the hangman when he writes that an execution was a normal event "comme la braisière du talmellier ou la tuerie de l'écorcheur. Le bourreau n'était qu'une espèce de boucher un peu plus foncé qu'un autre" (p. 388).

Similarly, Claude Frollo represents all the learned superstition of the age which, in Hugo's eyes, existed within the Church. His belief in fatality, ἀνάγκη, a non-Christian concept, denies liberty to the individual. Like a possessed man, he sees the trapping of a fly by a spider as symbolic of the human situation: "Elle [la mouche] vole, elle est joyeuse, elle vient de naître; elle cherche le printemps, le grand air, la liberté; oh! oui, mais qu'elle se heurte à la rosace fatale, l'araignée en sort, l'araignée hideuse!" (p. 323).[32] Claude sees himself as both fly and spider, victim of fate and agent of its designs. A representative of the Church, he has protected Quasimodo, harboring him in the cathedral but, at the same time, taking away his freedom. Quasimodo is the dog, says Hugo, Frollo, the master.

The monsterlike Quasimodo physically represents the misery of a society filled with the ugly. In the popular mind, Esmeralda's and Quasimodo's presence in the cathedral represents injustice, even though the hunchback has rescued and protected the gypsy in his one act of freedom. When the crowd attacks Notre-Dame near the end of the novel, it wishes only to destroy the symbols of ecclesiastical power. "Nous sommes des vaillants. Assiéger l'église, enfoncer les portes, en tirer la belle fille, la sauver des juges, la sauver des prêtres, démanteler le cloître, brûler l'évêque dans l'évêché, nous ferons cela en moins de temps qu'il n'en faut à un bourgmestre pour manger une cuillerée de soupe. Notre cause est juste" (pp. 458–59). Both Esmeralda and Quasimodo, once placed in Hugo's favorite antithesis of the *beau-laid* represent "les deux misères extrêmes de la nature et de la société qui se touchaient et qui s'entr'aidaient" (p. 403).

One of the most telling images of the novel communicates how hopeless Esmeralda's situation is when she is in prison. It is based on Dante and could describe the condition of most of fifteenth-century society as Hugo saw it. He takes up the image again in *Les Misérables* when he moves his social hell from the fifteenth to the nineteenth century.

> A la bastille Saint-Antoine, au Palais de Justice de Paris, au Louvre, ces édifices souterrains étaient des prisons. Les étages de ces prisons, en s'enfonçant dans le sol, allaient se rétrécissant

et s'assombrissant. C'étaient autant de zones où s'échelonnaient les nuances de l'horreur. Dante n'a rien pu trouver de mieux pour son enfer. Ces entonnoirs de cachots aboutissaient d'ordinaire à un cul de basse-fosse à fond de cuve où Dante a mis Satan, où la société mettait le condamné à mort. Une fois une misérable existence enterrée là, adieu le jour, l'air, la vie, *ogni speranza*. Elle n'en sortait que pour le gibet ou le bûcher. (P. 368)

The spiral image, associated previously with the fantastic aspects of medieval legend and with the psychology of both Hugo and his characters, has now been appropriated by Hugo's political and social conscience.

The architectural setting of the novel, particularly that of the cathedral, has received considerable attention from scholars and critics. It has been called the principal character or a magnet controlling the human characters.[33] Paul Zumthor has noted that Notre-Dame should also be seen as "type absolu de l'art-roi dont le poète s'est institué le découvreur."[34] Literary historians have praised Hugo's poetic translation of his antiquarian interest into word pictures of the church and the city,[35] and his personal "guerre aux démolisseurs" has been interpreted as "la pensée d'esthétique et de philosophie" which Hugo claimed to have hidden in the book (p. 6).[36] The architectural setting is also linked to the same historical, political, and social concerns that caused Hugo to develop the theme of the people and their future triumph in the novel.

From the attention devoted to gothic architecture in the 1826 preface to the *Odes et Ballades* and the 1829 introduction to the *Orientales*, it is clear that the gothic for Hugo meant the flamboyant — light, airy, and rich in detail. Although the grotesque was also central to his vision of medieval art, he invariably portrays the gothic style in this fixed way. When he turned to fifteenth-century Paris, however, he chose Notre-Dame cathedral, "une oeuvre de transition," to represent this society marked by flux and change. In the chapter devoted to the architecture of the church, Hugo says that it is not a definite, complete monument open to classification; it is situated between the romanesque and gothic. "Notre-Dame de Paris n'a point . . . la majestueuse simplicité des édifices qui ont le plein cintre pour générateur. Elle n'est pas, comme la cathédrale de Bourges, le produit magnifique, léger, multiforme, touffu, hérissé, efflorescent de l'ogive" (p. 130).

The discussion of gothic architecture continues but in different terms; it is called the second transformation, which terminated with William the Conqueror. For the first time, Hugo places the gothic in a political context by speaking of the family of churches in that style: "communales, et bourgeoises comme symboles politiques libres, capricieuses, effrénées, comme oeuvre d'art; seconde transformation de l'architecture, non plus hiéroglyphique, immuable et sacerdotale, mais artiste, progressive et populaire, qui commence au retour des croisades et finit à Louis XI" (p. 131).[37] Gothic architecture is seen as the free expression of a popular, progressive effort so that Hugo now has extended his more liberal stance into his interpretation of the gothic, politicizing it, in effect. Paradoxically, he portrays medieval society as something less than free, though the progressive freeing of architecture parallels the slow movement of the populace toward freedom. As a result, in this novel, Notre-Dame cathedral, "vaste symphonie en pierre," "produit prodigieux de la cotisation de toutes les forces d'une époque," "sorte de création," with its "sombre couleur des siècles," embodies, in part, the spirit of the late Middle Ages (pp. 126–27). It inspires both admiration and terror. The somber aspects are linked to Quasimodo, that other embodiment of the suffering people, so that the two are seen as outgrowths of the injustices in medieval history. Of Quasimodo's relationship to the cathedral, Hugo writes that "la cathédrale ne lui était pas seulement la société, mais encore l'univers, mais encore toute la nature." The richness of the gothic cathedral becomes the richness of nature and replaces the outside world for Quasimodo. "Il ne rêvait pas . . . d'autres montagnes que les tours colossales de l'église, d'autre océan que Paris qui bruissait à leurs pieds" (p. 180).

In viewing the city of Paris in the 1400s, Hugo was most impressed by the homogeneity and unity of its architecture. "Ce n'était pas alors seulement une belle ville; c'était une ville homogène, un produit architectural et historique du moyen âge, une chronique de pierre. C'était une cité formée de deux couches seulement, la couche romane et la couche gothique" (p. 158). Throughout the novel, however, this architectural unity is juxtaposed with the theme of historical change. Hugo the antiquarian who wished to preserve the monuments of the past may have admired the unity of the Paris of Louis XI, but he knew that the winds of social change were already leading to the Renaissance; a never-ending series of architectural changes would follow,[38] and Hugo viewed with horror any attempts to destroy the last vestiges of these past architectural eras. Paris was perhaps more beautiful, though less harmonious, fifty years later when renaissance architecture added "le luxe éblouissant de ses fantaisies et de ses systèmes" to the Paris of 1482. "Mais ce splendide moment dura peu. La renaissance ne fut pas impartiale; elle ne se contenta pas d'édifier, elle voulut jeter bas" (p. 158).

Hugo's sensitivity to historical change is most evident in the important chapter "Ceci tuera cela." Implicit in the development of his thought is the idea that humanity collectively expresses itself in some art form and that, from generation to generation, this mode of expression changes. Architecture had been the book of mankind up through the fifteenth century — "le grand livre de l'humanité, l'expression principale de l'homme à ses divers états de développement soit comme force, soit comme intelligence" (p. 210). Like writing, architecture evolved from alphabet to hieroglyphic to symbol until "l'idée mère, le verbe, n'était pas seulement au fond de tous ces édifices, mais encore dans la forme" (p. 211).[39] Hugo repeats his interpretation of the gothic as the expression of the people, and links the romanesque style to the hierarchical world of the Christian Middle Ages. The "style roman" reflects authority, unity, impenetrability, and the absolute, "partout la caste, jamais le peuple. Mais les croisades arrivent. C'est un grand mouvement populaire; et tout grand mouvement populaire, quels qu'en soient la cause et le but, dégage toujours de son dernier précipité l'esprit de liberté" (p. 213). The ogive, made possible by the liberating spirit of the crusades, is consequently the expression of freedom in architectural form, and it prefigures the inevitable movement toward popular freedom in politics and society. Everything begins to change and architecture is dethroned in the fifteenth century with Gutenberg's invention of printing; the book will kill the edifice. "L'invention de l'imprimerie est le plus grand événement de l'histoire. C'est la révolution mère. C'est le mode d'expression de l'humanité qui se renouvelle totalement" (p. 218). The sixteenth century thus becomes the age in which thought is emancipated, and this emancipation leads directly to Luther. Religious unity is broken, but printing makes reform possible. The tragedy of this inevitable historical development is that architecture as a collective expression disappears and a period of "décadence magnifique" ensues. "L'architecture ne sera plus l'art social, l'art collectif" (p. 222).

It is easy to see why Hugo continually juxtaposed the fifteenth and sixteenth centuries and why his attitude toward the late Middle Ages was ambivalent. He regretted that the individual was destined to replace the collective in artistic expression, for art would never again have the liberating force for a society that the gothic cathedral had for the medieval spirit. The stirrings of the masses and the disappearance of the feudal system, on the other hand, pave the way for the revolution of ideas in the sixteenth century. Although Hugo sees progress in history as inevitable, in *Notre-Dame* he does not advocate revolution per se. Rather, his belief in the power of the word as the embodiment of the ideal lies behind his admiration for the revolution within civilization during the Renaissance. This position represents Hugo's moderate liberalism of the 1830s, and it parallels his interpretation of the Revolution of 1789 in his essay on Mirabeau. There Hugo admires Mirabeau the orator because of his power with words and ideas, and he sees the revolution less in terms of politics than in terms of ideas. It lay the groundwork for all future progress so that Hugo conceives of his own century as the heir to the new ideas of that revolution. In his introductory essay to *Littérature et philosophie mêlées*, he says that progress in art is a corollary of social progress. But elsewhere, he again indicates that the goal toward which history is moving will be reached slowly but inevitably. "Cette oeuvre sera la formation paisible, lente et logique d'un ordre social où les principes nouveaux dégagés par la Revolution française trouveront enfin leur mode de combinaison avec les principes éternels et primordiaux de toute civilisation."[40] Hugo's admiration for the ideal and the power of the written word, evident in his comment that the book would kill the edifice, eventually led him to view his own imaginative creations with words as cathedrals.

> Rien avec la matière, tout dans l'idéal, c'est cela et cela seul qui fait la poésie supérieure à l'architecture. Sans doute, quand je m'arrête devant la façade de Notre Dame et que je me représente ces innombrables ouvriers . . . construisant assise par assise le prodigieux édifice sous le regard lumineux et fécondant de l'architecte, je me sens pénétré d'une inexprimable admiration, mais c'est plus que de l'adoration que j'éprouve, c'est un étonnement mêlé de religieuse adoration pour mon créateur quand, à l'aide de cet oeil intérieur qu'on nomme la rêverie, je vois au dedans de moi, fourmillement immense et tumultueux, ces autres ouvriers merveilleux, les pensées, qui avec des mots bâtissent une cathédrale dans mon esprit.[41]

History and Narrative Technique

Hugo's fascination with the historical process and with the recreation of the social and architectural milieu of medieval Paris has caused a number of critics to comment negatively about the organization of the novel. Hugo has been accused of trying for spectacular effects and of inaccuracy in his painting of the architecture of Notre-Dame and the vivid activities of the Cour des Miracles.[42] Raouf Simaïka notes that "l'idée de mettre en valeur certains chapitres purement documentaires, en faisant du roman une oeuvre 'spectaculaire,' donne, au détriment du récit, une importance de plus en plus grande à la peinture du passé. Les digressions, les dissertations, qui sont comme autant de monographies sur une époque moins bien étudiée qu'illustrée, sont un élément caractéristique du goût romantique. Mais il faut savoir gré à l'auteur d'avoir peint un moyen âge populaire et non féodal."[43] In a similar vein, Marius-François Guyard concludes that Hugo did not know how to choose between the historical novel, the novel of ideas, and the novel-poem.[44]

Understanding how Hugo attempted to give form to history and fictional narrative in *Notre-Dame de Paris* is useful in reaching a judgment about the aesthetic worth of the book. *Notre-Dame* defies classification, but Hugo did have definite ideas about the "historical novel" as a genre. His early statements about history and the novel were made in connection with Walter Scott; in the *Conservateur littéraire*, he praises Scott's fidelity to historical detail and coloring. This opinion is repeated in the well-known article on *Quentin Durward* in the *Muse française*. Hugo describes Scott as a "génie puissant et curieux qui devine le passé; pinceau vrai qui trace un portrait fidèle d'après une ombre confuse, et nous force à reconnaître même ce que nous n'avons pas vu."[45] In the conclusion to the article, Hugo calls for a new novel which will be both dramatic and epic; picturesque, but poetic; real, but ideal; true, but large in scope. Since Scott was a genius who could guess and reconstruct the past, Hugo probably thought of historical fidelity more as "reconstitution of atmosphere"[46] than as accuracy of detail. For this reason, the passage on local color from *La Préface de Cromwell*, cited earlier, is extremely important. Since local color had to permeate the literary work, it was much more than the picturesque. The poetic imagination transformed such detail into a unifying atmosphere for an entire work, in this case the novel. In describing his own method in *Notre-Dame*, Hugo says that he *painted* Paris during the fifteenth century — he evoked it through imaginative insights.

> C'est une peinture de Paris au XVe siècle et du quinzième siècle à propos de Paris. . . . Le livre n'a aucune prétention historique, si ce n'est dépeindre peut-être avec quelque science et quelque conscience, mais uniquement par aperçus et par échappées, l'état des moeurs, des croyances, des lois, des arts, de la civilisation enfin du XVe siècle. Au reste, ce n'est pas là ce qui importe dans le livre. S'il a un mérite, c'est d'être oeuvre d'imagination, de caprice et de fantaisie.[47]

Hugo does not always couple the narrative of the novel with the historical atmosphere. The principal characters are his own creations. In fact, much later in his career, he claimed never to have written a historical drama or novel. "Ma manière est de peindre des chose vraies par des personnages d'invention."[48] Further, the unifying principle is not found in a strict narrative sequence, but in contrast and scope (drama and epic). This aspect of Hugo's creativity in prose is often misunderstood, but it is simply an extension of his "unlimited lyricism," to use Thibaudet's phrase. The twentieth-century reader is left, then, with a melodramatic plot apparently derived from "gothic horror" as it existed both on the stage and in fiction. It appears to have relatively little to do with the historical atmosphere that provides a record in poetic form of how the nineteenth century perceived the Middle Ages. Historical atmosphere and plot do merge on occasion, however, when the narrator interrupts the story line or when the trio of main characters assumes a symbolic function within the fifteenth-century milieu.

Hugo the narrator is supremely conscious of his role in reconstituting the medieval past, and his intrusions into the narrative sequence reinforce the reader's sense of historical distance between his own era and that of the novel. In fact, the work begins with a hyperbole that emphasizes this passing of time. "Il y a aujourd'hui trois cent quarante-huit ans six mois et dix-neuf jours que les parisiens s'éveillèrent au bruit de toutes les cloches sonnant à grande volée dans la triple enceinte de la Cité, de l'Université et de la Ville. Ce n'est cependant pas un jour dont l'histoire ait gardé souvenir que le 6 janvier 1482" (p. 11). Hugo will make the day memorable for the nineteenth century, and thereafter he intervenes for many different reasons as he contrasts the two eras. From time to time, he underlines the stated purpose of the novel, to combat the destruction of the monuments of the Middle Ages, by recreating verbally a site which has already disappeared. An example is the Place de Grève. "Il ne reste aujourd'hui qu'un bien imperceptible vestige de la place de Grève telle qu'elle existait alors. C'est la charmante tourelle qui occupe l'angle nord de la place, et qui, déjà ensevelie sous l'ignoble badigeonnage qui empâte les vives arêtes de ses sculptures, aura bientôt disparu peut-être..." (p. 70). A long description of the Place de Grève as it once was follows.

At other times, Hugo emphasizes that the spirit which once animated the architecture of Paris has disappeared so that what remains is only a monument. The relationship between Quasimodo and Notre-Dame in the chapter "Immanis pecoris custos, immanior ipse" indicates that the animating spirit of the hunchback gives the cathedral its "fantastic, supernatural and horrible" aspect. Quasimodo is the "soul" of the cathedral. "A tel point que pour ceux qui savent que Quasimodo a existé, Notre-Dame est aujourd'hui déserte, inanimée, morte. On sent qu'il y a quelque chose de disparu. Ce corps immense est vide; c'est un squelette; l'esprit l'a quitté, on en voit la place, et voilà tout" (p. 184).

The narrator also interprets and judges the Middle Ages, and in these interpretations there is usually an implied comparison with the nineteenth century. Thus, when Louis XI comes in disguise with his doctor to visit Claude Frollo and a prologue of mutual flattery between the two "learned" men ensues, Hugo comments that the custom is still in existence as it was then. When Esmeralda's goat is put on trial along with his mistress, Hugo again adds an ironic commentary: "Rien de plus simple alors qu'un procès de sorcellerie intenté à un animal"; he then continues with documentation for his opinion (p. 356). Other examples could be cited, ranging from Hugo's explanation of why there were no police in the Paris of Louis XI to what constituted a place of asylum in the Middle Ages. The most striking example of historical distance to create irony is the treatment of the poet-philosopher Gringoire. Even though Gringoire is the author of the ill-fated mystery play and the object of abuse by the *truands,* he is treated with a tone of detachment so that he serves only a comic purpose. He seems to be a nineteenth-century character wearing medieval costume. For instance, when Gringoire decides to follow Esmeralda after the procession for the *fête des fous,* Hugo says that Gringoire acts from a vague desire to follow the train of events. "Si Gringoire vivait de nos jours, quel beau milieu il tiendrait entre le classique et le romantique!" (p. 86).

Most intrusions into the narration are direct addresses to the reader. Hugo may call on the reader to imagine the scene at hand. ("Maintenant, que ceux de nos lecteurs qui ont la puissance de généraliser une image et une idée, comme on dit dans le style d'aujourd'hui, nous permettent de leur demander s'ils se figurent bien nettement le spectacle qu' offrait, au moment où nous arrêtons leur attention, le vaste parallélogramme de la grand'salle du Palais" [p. 51].) In the second half of the novel, Hugo is usually reminding the reader of the narrative thread which has become obscured by the historical apparatus: "Que le lecteur nous permette de le remener," "Nos lecteurs n'ont pas oublié," "Le lecteur a sans doute déjà raconnu," "Le lecteur n'a peut-être pas oublié" (pp. 290, 332, 455).

This type of reminder is found in the second half of the novel, for these intrusions into the narrative indicate two concepts of time in *Notre-Dame.* On one hand, time is the Past, a vital period in history, recaptured, suspended in motion through aesthetic form; on the other hand, time is the actual measurable period of the events of the plot, a chronology unimportant to Hugo. The novel opens on the sixth of January 1482, a day he hopes to make memorable because the events occur that trigger the sequence of happenings comprising the "actual" time of the plot. But for five of the eleven books of the novel, Hugo has reduced the movement of the narrative sequence to slow motion; the date remains 6 January. In book six, actual time is speeded up; it is now 7 January. By book seven, March 1482, the sequence is further accelerated; book eight brings us to April, and thereafter events follow rapidly to a conclusion. Because of this division of the "actual" time, the reader's attention needs direction; the author's fascination with recapturing the vitality of an epoch overshadows the plot. These two concepts of time may pose problems if the reader looks for one "actual" narrative time. In analyzing Hugo's mature novelistic technique, Michel Butor has observed that what is characteristic of Hugo as novelist is "la violence avec laquelle il coupe ce fil [du récit]."[49] Hugo's text demands that the reader enter a special verbal construct or edifice representing an era before he is permitted to follow a fictional chain of events.

By breaking the thread of narration, Hugo establishes the historical atmosphere of the Past in books one through five of *Notre-Dame*. Butor has indicated that the "parenthesis" is one of the major ways the plot is interrupted. It is a pause for historical or poetical consideration which appears to be perpendicular to the anecdotal narration but is intimately connected with it.[50] The parenthesis enlarges the context of the anecdotal narrative and is typified by the chapter "Ceci tuera cela." Here, Hugo takes Claude Frollo's belief in fatality, removes it from the plane of his passion for Esmeralda, and transforms it in the theme of the inevitable changes under way in fifteenth-century society and art. The chapters "Notre-Dame" and "Paris à vol d'oiseau" are also outside the narrative sequence, but they enlarge the reader's understanding of the physical milieu. These two chapters in the first half of the novel follow the initial events and precede the fourth book, which contains a flashback to the previous history of Claude Frollo and Quasimodo; this ensures that the symbolic aspects of the cathedral are connected by the reader to the priest and the bell-ringer. Emphasis on unified architecture provides a contrast with the prophecy of change in the chapter "Ceci tuera cela" which follows the history of Frollo and Quasimodo.

Books one and two illustrate aspects of Hugo's technique that enhance the historical atmosphere and obscure the "actual" narrative time — even though the purpose of these chapters is to trigger the plot sequence. The novel begins with the presentation of Gringoire's mystery play before a huge crowd in the Palais de Justice; Quasimodo is the king to the fools, and Esmeralda makes her first appearance. The second book continues with Esmeralda's dance at the Place de Grève, Gringoire's attempt to follow Esmeralda, the aborted kidnaping of the gypsy, and the "marriage" of Esmeralda and Gringoire. In both sections, Hugo's dramatic-lyric bent dominates, and the crowd scenes with their raucousness and lively repartee overshadow the action of the main plot.

In some of Hugo's attempts to reconstitute a scene through words, his verbal creation seems to take over the page; the resulting aesthetic of expansive verbal dynamism matches the vitality of the popular age Hugo describes.[51] The crowd that is waiting for the beginning of the mystery play is compared with the movement of rising water, an image that is developed and expanded: "La foule s'épaississait à tout moment, et, comme une eau qui dépasse son niveau, commençait à monter le long des murs, à s'enfler autour des piliers, à déborder sur les entablements, sur les corniches, sur les appuis de fenêtres, sur toutes les saillies de l'architecture, sur tous les reliefs de la sculpture" (p. 19).

After completing the description of the crowd, Hugo proceeds with several pages of brilliant repartee that amplifies the medieval student milieu. A similar technique is used when he enumerates in detail each section of the parade of "underworld" figures during the *fête* (p. 81).

The physical environment is also vitalized by Hugo's amplifications. In one paragraph, he calls the Cour des Miracles a "cercle magique," "cité des voleurs, hideuse verrue à la face de Paris," "égout," "ruche monstrueuse," "hôpital menteur," and "immense vestiaire" (p. 97). "C'était une vaste place, irrégulière et mal pavée, comme toutes les places de Paris alors. Des feux, autour desquels fourmillaient des groupes étranges, y brillaient çà et là. Tout cela allait, venait, criait" (p. 97). The description continues, but the narrator's theme is clear: "tout semblait être en commun parmi ce peuple." All elements of human suffering and the consequent evils blend into one monstrous whole in the Cour des Miracles; and there is an interaction between the people and the Paris in which they are enclosed — when Paris becomes a seething mass of humanity, there is a superb union of style and theme.

Hugo's treatment of history and narrative indicates that he was not primarily concerned with presenting a chronicle of past events. A single "historical" occurrence, the arrival of a delegation in Paris to negotiate the marriage of Margaret of Flanders and the Dauphin, is a stage for the opening scenes of the novel. As in *Quentin Durward,* the characters with a basis in history, primarily Louis XI, are on the periphery of the plot. Claude Frollo may have been modeled on a historical archdeacon, but the character is closer to Ambrosio in Lewis's *The Monk.* Hugo does *use* history, however, and the architectural thesis that medieval monuments must be saved marks his book as propaganda, though it is more than that. Hugo's evocation of the collective sufferings of the people and of their self-expression in art interprets social and intellectual history in terms of his own political sympathies and marks a step toward his tendency after exile to use the Middle Ages overtly for political ends.

The central plot remains a tale of melodramatic horror, anchored here and there to the historical milieu and enhanced by "parentheses." The main characters of this plot rarely derive motivation for their actions from their milieu, nor are there frequent attempts to see why they act as they do; for these reasons there is a basic unevenness in Hugo's handling of history and narrative in *Notre-Dame de Paris.* Often he relies on the use of animal imagery to describe a character instead of analyzing his or her inner thoughts and feelings. Throughout the novel, for instance, Esmeralda is referred to as a bird or small, helpless creature. Such images are numerous at the beginning of the book where she is introduced as a wasp (p. 75), a nightingale (p. 79), a cicada (p. 80), and a warbler (p. 89). Like Hugo's other female figures, she becomes a fixed, fragile, and idealized type. Later, when she is threatened, she becomes the fly caught in the spider's web of fate (pp. 323, 369, 562). Quasimodo cannot be compared easily with anything of the animal realm, for he is half monster himself — a Polyphemus or a Cyclops (pp. 63, 90, 269). When the two creatures are in the cathedral, Quasimodo refuses at first to enter Esmeralda's room, sensing that she recoils before his ugliness. "Non, non . . . le hibou n'entre pas dans le nid de l'alouette" (p. 422). Then he gives an uncharacteristic statement of his own feelings about his ugliness; this is one of the few times we see into his character: "— Moi, je suis quelque chose d'affreux, ni homme, ni animal, un je ne sais quoi plus dur, plus foulé aux pieds et plus difforme qu'un caillou!" (p. 422).

The omniscient narrator, so knowledgeable in most things, often disavows any insight into the inner thoughts and emotions of his characters. When Quasimodo rings the bells of Notre-Dame and feels the "monsters of bronze" vibrate, he is called "un étrange centaure moitié homme, moitié cloche" (p. 183). But the narrator refuses to analyze Quasimodo's emotions; he indicates that he is unable to explore "this opaque creature" (p. 179).

The same technique is applied to Claude Frollo in the chapter "Utilité des fenêtres qui donnent sur la rivière" in which we find the priest hidden behind a door as Phoebus and Esmeralda are about to arrive for their assignation. The narrator gives all his attention to the priest at the beginning of the chapter, only to tell the reader that he is unable to analyze the priest's emotions and thoughts. "Que se passait-il en ce moment dans l'âme obscure de l'archidiacre? lui et Dieu seul l'ont pu savoir" (p. 339). When the two lovers enter the room, we immediately abandon Claude to follow the sensational scene between Phoebus and Esmeralda. We return behind the door when the narrator presents us with the image of the tormented face of the lascivious priest. "Qui eût pu voir en ce moment la figure du malheureux collée aux barreaux vermoulus eût cru voir une face de tigre regardant du fond d'une cage quelque chacal qui dévore une gazelle" (p. 345). After the narrator comes back to the seduction scene, he gives one final view of the priest from the point of view of Esmeralda as she glimpses the livid face of Claude behind Phoebus. "La jeune fille resta immobile, glacée, muette sous l'épouvantable apparition, comme une colombe qui lèverait la tête au moment où l'orfraie regarde dans son nid avec ses yeux ronds" (p. 347).[52]

With this one-dimensional characterization, events happen to Quasimodo, Esmeralda, and Claude Frollo, but there is no effect on their fixed personalities; symbolic functions are spelled out directly as parallels between these figures and their historical milieu.[53] Quasimodo and Esmeralda may stand for the extremes of misery in nature and society, but the connection between the fatal passion of Frollo for Esmeralda and the sufferings of the masses within the inevitable movement of history seems tenuous. Still, *Notre-Dame* marks an improvement over *Han d'Islande* where the exotic setting was a picturesque décor and no attempt was made to join this setting to the narrative sequence involving Ethel and Ordener. In the later novels, when Hugo has shed the last vestiges of the *roman noir,* there is a more complete union of history and narrative.

5

The Years 1832 to 1842

The Decade after Notre-Dame de Paris

A hiatus of about ten years separates the publication of *Notre-Dame de Paris* and the next major works by Hugo in which the Middle Ages are prominent. Although three volumes of poetry appeared during this decade, most of Hugo's energies were devoted to the theater. In almost every case, the settings of plays like *Le Roi s'amuse, Lucrèce Borgia, Marie Tudor, Angelo, La Esmeralda,* and *Ruy Blas* are in the sixteenth century as though Hugo had already moved effortlessly from the late Middle Ages of *Notre-Dame* to the century of the "Satyre," preeminent in *La Légende des Siècles.* When he did turn to medieval motifs for *Les Burgraves,* he centered his interest for the first time on the thirteenth century. The first edition of that play indicates just how conscious Hugo was of the historical settings of his works because opposite the title page he gives a chronology by century and country of everything he had published until that time.[1] He begins with *Les Burgraves* in the thirteenth century, followed by *Notre-Dame de Paris* in the fifteenth century; five works are listed for the sixteenth century, four for the seventeenth, one for the eighteenth, and eleven for the nineteenth. Hugo's sensitivity to the movement of history was expanding to include a vision of the panorama of all civilization. Needless to say, the importance of the Middle Ages diminished when he turned to the entire scope of history.

Aside from his activities as a member of the Comité des Arts et Monuments, concerned with the preservation and restoration of the architecture of France, Hugo remains aloof in his imaginative writings of the 1830s from the medieval revival which *Notre-Dame de Paris* helped to create. Augustin Challamel discusses at some length the medieval rage of the 1830s in his *Souvenirs d'un hugolâtre* and gives special emphasis to the effect of Hugo's novel on Parisian society. "Effectivement, personne ne passait devant la cathédrale sans peupler, par l'imagination, ses tours imposantes, — sans songer à Claude et à Jehan Frollo, à Quasimodo et à Esmeralda."[2] Novels such as Roger de Beauvoir's *L'Ecolier de Cluny* and Alphonse Royer's *Mauvais Garçons* and *Venezia la Bella* appeared and Meyerbeer's opera *Robert-le-Diable* was performed in 1831 with tremendous success. Dumas's plays *Henri III* and *La Tour de Nesle* were paralleled by Casimir Delavigne's *Marino Faliero* and *Louis XI*. In the Latin Quarter, the "chapeau à la Buridan" was worn by enthusiasts of the Middle Ages, and in general, people began to dress like the characters of Hugo's and Dumas's plays. "Medieval" dress essentially meant a *mode* combining elements of the fourteenth, fifteenth, and sixteenth centuries.[3] This same mixing of earlier styles held sway in furnishings. In *Les Vignettes romantiques,* Champfleury comments that "ce fut alors, dans les appartemens à la mode, un pêle-mêle de moyen âge et de Renaissance."[4] By the mid-1830s the public had adopted the Middle Ages, but this was a different taste from that of the Empire or early Restoration — the grotesque, the fantastic, and gothic bric-à-brac replaced Marchangy and the genre troubadour.

Although Hugo may not have given much attention to the Middle Ages in the late 1830s he did adopt, in *Les Voix intérieures,* the figures of Dante and Dürer as symbols of the visionary artist who through *contemplation* or *rêverie* penetrates to a different level of reality and recreates the fantastic world of vision in art. Already in 1830, Hugo was using the image of the spiral to describe the visionary process as one of descent in "La Pente de la rêverie": "Une pente invisible/ Va du monde réel à la sphere invisible."[5] During the years of exile, Hugo applied the image to himself as the instrument of descent, no longer limiting it to the poetic process alone. "Moi qu'on nomme le poëte,/ Je suis dans la nuit muette/ L'escalier mystérieux."[6]

Hugo also expanded his description of *contemplation* to include three kinds of processes: observation, imagination, and intuition. "L'observation s'applique plus spécialement à l'humanité, l'imagination à la nature, l'intuition au surnaturalisme. Par l'observation, le poëte est philosophe, et peut être législateur; par l'imagination, il est mage, et créateur; par l'intuition, il est prêtre, et peut être révélateur."[7] In *Les Voix intérieures,* Dante and Dürer are artists of imagination, and implicitly, extensions of Hugo himself. At Heidelburg in 1840, Hugo could ask: "Etes-vous visionnaire comme moi? Avez-vous éprouvé cela? Les statues dorment le jour; mais, la nuit, elles se réveillent et deviennent fantômes."[8] This statement is only the culmination of the process by which Hugo's observations of the details of architecture and of the "picturesque" in nature matured during his yearly trips after 1834. As a result, Hugo's created world — the vision he put in prose and poetry — also parallels, in his mind, the *Inferno* of Dante and the fantastic forests of Dürer.[9]

Hugo's increasing fascination with Dante goes far beyond the interest he had first expressed in *La Préface de Cromwell.* How much of the *Divine Comedy* he had read is subject to debate despite the title of the poem of 1836, "Après une lecture de Dante." Although he knew the Rivarol and La Mennais translations of the *Comedy*,[10] a likely source for the poem at this time is the 1829 translation by Antoni Deschamps of twenty of the most striking cantos along with illustrative lithographs. As a member of Hugo's *cénacle*, Deschamps had cited the spokesman for Romanticism in his preface. About the demons of Malbowges in cantos 21 and 22 of the *Inferno*, he writes that "Dante consacre deux chants à la peinture de ces démons et à leurs querelles; c'est la partie *comique* du poème, c'est le grotesque, cet élément nécessaire de toute grande composition moderne, comme le dit Victor Hugo dans son admirable préface de Cromwell."[11]

Hugo would also have appreciated Deschamps's evaluation of the *Comedy* as an original epic embodying the fourteenth century. "*La Divine Comédie* est originale dans le fond et dans la forme, . . . certes le livre de Dante est une admirable épopée, la plus admirable que nous connaissons; Dante, c'est le moyen âge italien qui s'est fait homme."[12] Deschamps assumes that both Dante the man *and* the poetic masterpiece of Dante the poet embody his age; the grotesque is also an extension of Dante's own society with all its conflicts and of the contradictions within the poet: "ses croyances, sa superstition, sa physique, sa poésie, sa scolastique, ses guerres civiles, son républicanisme féodal, si différent du républicanisme antique."[13] Sainte-Beuve also repeats this general view of the grotesque parts of the *Comedy* in a tribute to Deschamps which indicates the importance of his translation among the Romantics. "Dante est un puissant maître, à l'allure hardie,/ Dont j'adore à genoux l'étrange Comédie./ Mais le sentier est rude et tourne à l'infini,/ Et j'attends, pour monter, notre guide Antony."[14]

There are three clear divisions within "Après une lecture de Dante." Hugo begins the poem with a statement regarding the relationship between the poet and the world he creates: "Quand le poète peint l'enfer, il peint sa vie."[15] A series of images follows, describing this "life" in terms of the creative act, a movement of descent on a ramp that disappears into mist. "Noir voyage obstrué de rencontres difformes;/ Spirale aux bords douteux, aux profondeurs énormes,/ Dont les cercles hideux vont toujours plus avant/ Dans une ombre où se meut l'enfer vague et vivant!" The poetic descent of a Dante has immediately been placed in the general context of all imaginative vision. Since the imagery is also customarily used by Hugo to describe his personal creative process, the reader can assume that both Dante and Hugo are archetypes of the imaginative poet of genius.

Hugo's identification with the figure of Dante — rather than his specific knowledge of the *Inferno* — is also illustrated in the second division of the poem. Here a series of fleeting glimpses of the *visions*, *rêves*, and *chimères* in the world to which the poet has descended is developed, but the only identifiable figures from the *Inferno* are Paolo, Francesca, and Ugolin. "L'amour, couple enlacé, triste, et toujours brûlant,/ Qui dans un tourbillon passe une plaie au flanc;/ Dans un coin la vengeance et la faim, soeurs impies,/ Sur un crâne rongé côte à côte accroupies." Both these episodes were commonplaces in Romantic discussions of Dante.

Although Hugo began by concentrating on the relation between the poem and the poet in the first line of "Après une lecture," in the concluding lines the poet's vision becomes generalized. "Oui, c'est bien là la vie, ô poète inspiré,/ Et son chemin brumeux d'obstacles encombré." The poetic creation, a result of the individual's vision, becomes universal once it has been given artistic form. And if the writer often perceives the darker, shadowy aspect of life, as did Dante, he must also emphasize the positive facet, and for this reason Virgil, "le génie au front calme," leads the way in Dante's poem.[16]

In "A Albert Durer" (1837), Hugo pays homage to another visionary: "ton oeil visionnaire/ Voyait distinctement."[17] The personalized interpretation of Dürer is in marked contrast with the earlier "Un Dessin d'Albert Dürer — Minuit"; after recreating the strange world of the "vieilles forêts" as envisioned by Dürer, Hugo associates himself, in the final lines, with this mode of perception and creation. "Aux bois, ainsi que toi, je n'ai jamais erré,/ Maître, sans qu'en mon coeur l'horreur ait pénétré." Hugo seems to have known Dürer primarily via his copper engravings *Knight, Death and Devil* and *Melancholia I,* but the subject matter of the poem is important, for it marks Hugo's developing interest in Germany.

As André Monchoux has demonstrated, French intellectual circles began to discover and understand German thought and culture during the years 1814 through 1835,[18] but Hugo's portrayal of Germany rests on the level of poetic evocation and remains limited by his Rhine trip of 1840.[19] The technique of this poem on Dürer indicates well how Hugo projected the characteristics of an era, a country, or a landscape onto symbolic figures. This technique would be used in *Le Rhin,* but here it means that Dürer is Hugo and, at the same time, the "incarnation de la Forêt germanique."[20] Yet, the forest, though animated, somber, and fantastic, is not quite the woods of the "Chevalier de la Mort" or the identifiable locale of *Le Rhin.* Dürer's forest is "un monde hideux," and Hugo chooses to bring it to life, showing it to be situated halfway between dream and reality. "Là se penchent rêveurs les vieux pins, les grands ormes/ Dont les rameaux tordus font cent coudes difformes,/ Et dans ce groupe sombre agité par le vent/ Rien n'est tout à fait mort ni tout à fait vivant."

One other significant allusion to Dürer in the poetry of 1837 accords him a symbolic function as historical link between the fifteenth and sixteenth centuries. In the concluding section of "Que la musique date du seizième siècle," Hugo contrasts the "vieux soleil gothique" with music, "cette lune de l'art." He mourns the death of the cathedral in the ferment of the sixteenth century, but celebrates the rise of music: ". . . Sereine, et blanchissant de sa lumière pure/ Ton dôme merveilleux, ô sainte Architecture,/ Dans ce ciel, qu'Albert Dure admirait à l'écart,/ La Musique montait, cette lune de l'art!"[21] There is no doubt that Hugo's admiration for gothic architecture remained constant while his sensitivity to the importance of the sixteenth century for the modern world evolved. The concept "gothic" had achieved so much importance that it becomes a synonym for all that is important in medieval art. The reference to Dürer's *Melancholia,* coming just one month after the writing of "A Albert Durer," suggests the Dürer, like Rabelais, had become for Hugo a transitional figure between the Middle Ages and the Renaissance.

The decade of the 1830s saw the rise of Hugo's interest in politics which has a direct bearing on the use of the Middle Ages in his imaginative writings.[22] With the government's suppression of *Le Roi s'amuse* in 1832, his antipathy to the existing constitutional monarchy became fixed, though his "liberalism" at this point did not extend to a complete endorsement of democratic political institutions. The preface to *Ruy Blas* is indicative of Hugo's sensitivity to historical change and to popular or liberal causes. Ruy Blas symbolizes the people in the crumbling monarchy of Charles II, and Hugo insists on the historical significance of his drama because he wishes to contrast the promise of the emperor Charles V's reign in *Hernani* with the situation in *Ruy Blas.* Repeating the images of the monologue of Don Carlos in act four of *Hernani,* Hugo comments that "on voit remuer dans l'ombre quelque chose de grand, de sombre et d'inconnu. C'est le peuple." The future, not the present, belongs to the masses.

Hugo was a Bonapartist during this period, and for this reason evinced great enthusiasm for Charlemagne, Frederick Barbarossa, and Napoleon — the great emperors of the past. His "Discours de réception" at the Académie française has been described as "the piquant picture of a Bonapartist coming to rest in the Orléanist camp" because of its evocation of the national glories of Napoleonic France.[23] Hugo actively cultivated the support of the Duc d'Orléans before the Duke's death in 1842 and of the Duke's wife, Hélène de Mecklenbourg-Schwerin. Indeed, both *Le Rhin* and *Les Burgraves* can be attributed in part to Hugo's desire to influence the political crisis of the early 1840s. In 1840 the strong feeling in France for war with Prussia, a result of the treaty between England, Austria, Prussia, and Russia, gave support to Turkey in its conflict with Egypt.[24] Rebirth of the Napoleonic cult coincided both with the return of the emperor's remains and the sentiment for war. When Hugo went to Germany in 1840 he was aligned with the bellicose elements in France, but after his entry into the French Academy the following year, when he attempted to carve out a role for himself as a statesman, he no longer wished to be strongly anti-Prussian. Therefore he deleted the anti-Prussian statements from his letters and added political proposals to *Le Rhin* before its publication. Hugo supports the union of Germany and France against the supposed threat of England and Russia and proposes that France be given the left bank of the Rhine; these ideas clearly align him with the Duc d'Orléans.

> Dieu veut la grande France et la grande Allemagne.
> Il fit Napoléon comme il fit Charlemagne,
> Pour donner à l'Europe un centre souverain.
> Que Stamboul meure, alors vers l'orient tournée,
> Teutonia, de gloire et de paix couronée,
> Reprendre le Danube et nous rendra le Rhin![25]

The Legendary Rhine

Previous travelers to the Rhine, such as Musset and Dumas, had already published accounts of their excursions when Hugo made his trips in 1839 and 1840.[26] Hugo was, as a result, conscious of the literary as well as the political consequences of the publication of his letters. His introduction and conclusion clarify his political intentions, but he also attends to the form of the work. He claims that "cet ouvrage, qui a un fleuve pour sujet, s'est par une coïncidence bizarre, produit lui-même tout spontanément et tout naturellement à l'image d'un fleuve."[27] Since the letters were reorganized and edited, there is, despite Hugo's disclaimer, an overriding unity — a preoccupation with legend and history — suggested by the image of the river. In addition, the principle behind the form of *Le Rhin* is the same unity in variety Hugo saw in the gothic cathedral and the world of nature. "Je l'ai dit quelque part, l'unité dans la variété, c'est le principe de tout art complet. Sous ce rapport, la nature est la plus grande artiste qu'il y ait" (p. 264).

Hugo made his trips in 1839 and 1840,[28] armed with two standard books used by the tourists of the period, Schreiber's *Manuel des voyageurs sur le Rhin* and *Traditions populaires du Rhin.*[29] Both volumes had been translated from the German, and the first had appeared in five French editions by 1841. (Hugo knew the fourth.) Though other sources were used in the writing of *Le Rhin,* Schreiber is responsible for causing Hugo to cultivate "cette habitude de voir les paysages à travers les légendes."[30] In terms of Hugo's interest in legend and history, the published letters which deal with the trip actually made in 1840 are the key portion of the book. They show Hugo's progression from the guidebook reader who notes the legend connected with each medieval monument to the poet-visionary who claims legend and legendary ruins as his own possessions, for he has seen them come to life. This progression from guidebook reader to visionary is not spontaneous; in Paris Hugo added several sections dealing with legend to underscore his conception of past continuity impinging upon present experience.[31]

At Aix-la-Chapelle and Cologne, one would expect the descriptive method of Hugo the antiquarian; a concern for striking architectural detail and historical background prevails. However, he already shows an interest in the legend and the architecture of the church at Aix. How he incorporates this legend into his narrative is of particular interest. Hugo begins with a systematic description of the Palatine chapel, starting at the portal. Then he relates the tale that when the chapel was first under construction lack of funds threatened the project after just six months. The devil, in disguise, offered to provide the needed money in exchange for the first soul crossing the threshold. The offer was accepted, but the townspeople, in order to trick the devil, arranged for a wolf to be the first living being to enter the church. This legend is merely a parenthesis to the actual description of the church in letter nine, and Hugo introduces it as such. "(Pardon, mon ami, mais permettez-moi d'ouvrir une parenthèse. . . .)"[33] With so little integration into the fabric of the narrative, the story remains a curiosity piece.

In letter fifteen, the treatment of legend changes considerably; Hugo has begun to visit the ruins along the Rhine. The preceding letter, in discussing the Rhine as a river whose history symbolizes civilization, prepares the reader for this change in tone. Of the various phases of civilization on the Rhine, the age following initial Roman domination and barbarian invasions — the Dark Ages to some nineteenth-century historians — Hugo labels "une période merveilleuse." Civilization seemed to fall, sure traditions were lost, and history appeared to be obliterated. "Les hommes et les événements de cette sombre époque traversèrent le Rhin comme des ombres. . . . Les fables végètent, croissent, s'entremêlent et fleurissent dans les lacunes de l'histoire écroulée, comme les aubépines et les gentianes dans les crevasses d'un palais en ruine" (pp. 115–16). A long, evocative list follows of the mythic, fairy, and legendary figures of this period when imaginary tale replaced history.[34] Among the shadows, Hugo notes a number of "héros humains, presque aussi fantastiques que les personnages surnaturels," who have become legends and are symbolized by Dürer's knight.

Tous ces aventuriers, à demi enfoncés dans l'impossible et tenant à peine par le talon à la vie réelle, vont et viennent dans les légendes, perdus vers le soir dans les forêts inextricables, cassant les ronces et les épines, comme le *Chevalier de la mort* d'Albert Durer, sous le pas de leur cheval, suivis de leur lévrier efflanqué, regardés entre deux branches par des larves, et accostant dans l'ombre tantôt quelque noir charbonnier assis près d'un feu, qui est Satan entassant dans un chaudron les âmes des trépassés. (P. 117)

Enumeration of types of adventures (meetings with beautiful nymphs, little old men, or a powerful dwarf) continues, and, as in the theory of the grotesque, Hugo conveys the dark side of the medieval mind which necessarily gave birth to legend. He takes little interest in the iconographic details of Dürer's engraving, concentrating instead on the knight as an adventurer who belongs to two worlds, that of the impossible and that of real life. Nietzsche saw in the engraving "a symbol of our existence"; Hugo, too, saw a symbolic value in it, but he incorporated it into his own interpretation of the role of the *chevalier*. [35]

Beginning with letter fifteen, we view a series of ruins in terms of their legends, for "les ruines font vivre les contes, et les contes le leur rendent" (p. 175). At Velmich, the ruin called La Souris is placed in a sinister setting, and then Hugo recounts the legend of the cruel Falkenstein who, according to his own whim, threw people into the well of the castle; one day he ordered the local priest to be thrown into the water with the church bell tied to his neck. The priest pleaded with Falkenstein to give back the bell, which had been stolen. As retribution for such wicked actions, Falkenstein himself suddenly became ill, and the silver bell tolled his death knell from the depths of the well.

Although Hugo disassociates himself from the superstitions of the peasants, he does become a part of the atmosphere of sinister legend he has created. When he suddenly catches sight of the ruin in its savage isolation, the impression is so vivid that he expects the tower to be inhabited. "En cet instant-là, la forteresse éventrée m'est apparue avec un aspect si délabré et une figure si formidable et si sauvage, que j'avoue que je n'aurais pas été surpris le moins du monde de voir sortir de dissous les rideaux de lierre quelque forme surnaturelle portant des fleurs bizarres dans son tablier, Gela, la fiancée de Barberousse, ou Hildegarde, la femme de Charlemagne" (p. 127). Finally, Hugo recounts why the castle was called ironically "The Mouse"; it was the replacement of a smaller, weaker castle which had long been threatened by a larger, stronger fortification nearby named "The Cat." "*Die Mause* [sic] ... est encore une sinistre et redoutable commère sortie jadis armée et vivante, avec ses hanches de lave et de basalte, des entrailles mêmes de ce volcan éteint" (p. 130).

In letter sixteen, Hugo relates how he could not tear himself away from the ruin and thought of the Falkenstein legend as he listened at the wall and heard, by coincidence, the angelus bell of a far-off village. When at last he walks toward the nearby village of Saint-Goar as evening falls, the silence of the countryside induces a profound feeling of melancholy in the traveler. "Je n'avais plus au-dessus de moi qu'un de ces ciels de plomb où plane, visible pour le poète, cette grande chauve-souris qui porte écrit dans son ventre ouvert *melancholia*" (p. 133). In this instance, an exact detail from Dürer's engraving *Melancholia I* expresses Hugo's mood as opposed to the symbolic interpretation given to the "Chevalier de la Mort." One is reminded, also, of Nerval's use of detail from the same engraving in the opening quatrain of "El Desdichado." "Ma seule étoile est morte, — et mon luth constellé/ Porte le soleil noir de la Mélancolie." Hugo's melancholy mood at the hour of dusk is of great interest, for "l'heure crépusculaire" was often the moment when his imaginative vision, in conjunction with the changing light, transformed the natural world and penetrated the realm of appearances. Here, melancholy ensues when all light is blacked out, and his imagination (which functioned in terms of contrasts of lighting) is dormant.

In the descriptions of letter seventeen, entitled "Saint-Goar", history and legend exist on an equal footing. The ruin Le Chat does not impress Hugo in the same way La Souris had. "Aujourd'hui, *die Katz* est une belle ruine dont l'usufruit est loué par le duc de Nassau à un major prussien quatre ou cinq florins par an. Trois ou quatre visiteurs paient la rente" (p. 135). The natural setting of the castle, at the edge of the gorge called the "Bank," is more impressive than the ruin. "Entre la Bank et la tour carrée de Saint-Goarshausen, il n'y a qu'un passage étroit. D'un côté le gouffre, de l'autre l'écueil. On trouve tout sur le Rhin, même Charybde et Scylla" (p. 135). Farther on, Hugo marvels at the echo of the "fabuleux rocher de Lurley" (p. 136) and the Reichenberg. "C'est là que vivait, pendant les guerres du droit manuel du moyen âge, un des plus redoutables entre ces chevaliers-bandits qui se surnommaient eux-mêmes fléaux du pays (*landsschaden*)" (p. 137). Near the Reichenberg are the ruins of the "village des Barbiers," so Hugo must recount the story that all the barbers of Bacharach were carried off to that town when the devil planned to have Frederick Barbarossa shaved by a local Delilah.

The visit to the Rheinfels climaxes this potpourri of legend and history. "Toute une montagne évidée à l'intérieur avec des crêtes de ruines sur sa tête; deux ou trois étages d'appartements et de corridors souterrains qui paraissent avoir été creusés par des taupes colossales; d'immenses décombres; . . . un palais féodal des landgraves de Hesse changé en énorme masure" (pp. 138–39). Hugo is again overcome by melancholy, but this time it is produced by his consideration of the ruins of the Rheinfels in the perspective of time. Napoleon had over-thrown the fortress in 1807; only the four walls of the chapel remain, and the inscriptions provide a reminder of the small place man holds in history. "On ne traverse pas sans une certaine émotion mélancolique ce lieu de paix préservé seul au milieu de cette effrayante citadelle bouleversée. Dans les embrasures des fenêtres on lit ces graves inscrip-tions, deux par chaque fenêtre: *Sanctus Franciscus de Paula vixit 1500*. *Sanctus Franciscus vixit 1526*" (p. 139). These few inscriptions are all that remain after the incursions of war. In contrast with the legends that survived when barbarian invasions wiped out historical tradition, little of "la chaîne des traditions certaines" can outlive the self-destructiveness of modern man.

Other references to medieval legend and history follow. Bacharach, "ce vieux bourg-fée," is said to be occupied "par une population d'habitants pittoresques, qui tous . . . ont dans le regard, dans le profil et dans la tournure, je ne sais quels airs du treizième siècle" (p. 143, letter eighteen). For Hugo the ruins at Falkenberg evoke the story of Guntram, fiancé of Liba, who fell under the spell of Erlinde, spirit of the dead daughter of Bodo, lord of a mysterious château. As Guntram was leading his bride to the altar, in front of him were a knight dressed in black and a veiled woman visible to him alone. "Il sentit tout à coup une main froide dans la sienne, — la main de la pucelle du château de la forêt, qui se peignait la nuit en chantant près d'un tombeau ouvert et vide. — C'est dans cette salle basse qu'il expira et que Liba mourut de le voir mourir" (pp. 174–75).

The entire series of ruined châteaux culminates with Hugo's de-scription of the Maüsethurm in letter twenty. In chapter 3, I indicated that the visionary technique by which the poet animates a ruin and situates it in a sinister world reached a peak in Hugo's portrayal of the tower of Hatto. Hugo's celebrated sketch of the Maüsethurm, isolated in a murky Rhine against the backdrop of a turbulent sky, with the black outline of the castle of Bingen on the right, is a companion piece to his word picture.[36] The legend of the Maüsethurm in which he describes how the archbishop Hatto was eaten by rats in the isolated tower after having burned alive the starving populace of Mayence marks his complete identification with this legendary region of the Rhine. To introduce the legend he invents an anecdote from his childhood and claims that he is now reliving a childhood experience in which he was haunted in his dreams by a picture of just such a tower hanging above his bed. "La tour grandissait, l'eau bouillonnait, un éclair tombait des nuées, le vent sifflait dans les montagnes et semblait par moments jeter des clameurs. Un jour, je demandai à la servante comment s'appelait cette tour. Elle me répondait, en faisant un signe de croix, la Maüsethurm" (p. 176).

As if to give final proof of his affinity for German legend, Hugo inserts into the itinerary of his journey his own "Légende du Beau Pécopin" in letter twenty-one. There is a complete contrast in tone, which sets this "literary" legend apart from the preceding material. Hugo handles with consummate irony the tale of Pécopin's travels, his escape from the clutches of the devil by means of a talisman which also preserves his youth, his participation in an infernal hunt and feast at a magic castle, and his return to his fiancée Bauldour — only to find her to be a wasted old woman. Pécopin accidentally loses his talisman, and he also becomes aged. Although patterns for the main incidents can be found in Schreiber's collection and Nerval's translation of Bürger's "Féroce Chasseur," and many of the exotic details are borrowed from Rocoles's edition of the seventeenth-century encyclopedia, *Le Monde,* of Davity, Hugo's handling of his borrowed material is unique.[37] The irony of the "Légende du Beau Pécopin" indicates that Hugo could distance himself from the antiquarian-tourist framework of *Le Rhin* and therefore keep his documentary "persona" from appearing overly zealous. This legend seems Voltairian in its ironic understatement, its exotic details, and its serial adventures. The innocent hero resembles a Candide, but the philosophic overtones are missing from this narrative.[38] "Le beau Pécopin aimait la belle Bauldour, et la belle Bauldour aimait le beau Pécopin. Pécopin était fils du burgrave de Sonneck, et Bauldour était fille du sire de Falkenburg. L'un avait la forêt, l'autre avait la montagne. Or quoi de plus simple que de marier la montagne à la forêt? Les deux pères s'entendirent, et l'on fiança Bauldour à Pécopin" (p. 186). As if to reinforce the ironic tone, the medievalism of the "Légende du Beau Pécopin," like that of the *Ballades,* has no basis in actual history or culture but is part of the narrator's taste for the fantastic and the supernatural. This taste is all-inclusive, taking in such diverse elements as sylphs, fairies, German castles, and the exotic Orient.

Paul Zumthor interprets the "Légende" as a pastiche, though he thinks the central portion, "la chasse infernale" (chapters 10–12), is closely associated with the imagery of the rest of *Le Rhin.*[39] It is certainly true that the "chasse infernale" is the key portion of the tale which links it to the atmosphere of the rest of *Le Rhin.* But even in the concentrated imagery of these particular passages, ironic technique unifies the whole. In creating the chase through the "bois des pas perdus," Hugo gives free rein to his Rabelaisian taste for verbal catalogues, just as he has elsewhere in the legend, and he thereby gives a dense texture to the narrative thread. Given the character of Pécopin, a one-dimensional figure swept along by his adventures, the reader can easily see ironic tones in a passage of such verbal density as the following:

Galop rude, violent, rapide, étincelant, vertigineux, sur-
naturel, qui saisit Pécopin, qui l'entraîna, qui l'emporta, qui
faisait résonner dans son cerveau tous les pas du cheval comme
si son crâne eût été le pavé du chemin, qui l'éblouissait comme
un éclair, qui l'enivrait comme une orgie, qui l'exaspérait
comme une bataille; galop qui, par moments, devenait tourbillon, tourbillon qui parfois devenait ouragan. (P. 209)

From time to time, Pécopin reacts in a fashion that can only be taken
ironically. "Dans ces moments si terribles, ce doit être un grand effort
et c'est, à coup sûr, un grand mérite que de jeter son âme jusqu'à Dieu
et son coeur jusqu'à sa maîtresse. C'est ce que faisait dévotement le
brave chevalier. Il songeait donc au bon Dieu et à Bauldour, plus
encore peut-être à Bauldour qu'au bon Dieu" (p. 210). Pécopin is a
Candide placed in a mock-legendary world.

If Hugo was conscious of the Rhine's legendary past, he also was
interested in its history, but his "method" was that of a poet-
antiquarian, using a few significant details to create a past which lives
for the nineteenth century. "J'ai recueilli çà et là quelques dates
caractéristiques, quelques cailloux roulés dans le torrent des faits.
Usez-en pour reconstruire la figure du passé."[40] Despite the fact that
Hugo began to write a history of the Rhine for which he used sources
such as Pfeffel's *Nouvel abrégé chronologique de l'histoire et droit public en
Allemagne* (1776) and Kohlrausch's *Histoire d'Allemagne depuis les temps
les plus reculés* and the resources of libraries which he claimed to have
frequented while in Germany, he remained a dilettante. His reading
provided the numerous historical allusions that fill *Le Rhin,* and also
provided material for *Les Burgraves.*[41] Only two letters, numbers
fourteen and twenty-five, focus on the history of the river, though not
in any organized way. These chapters begin and conclude the series of
descriptions of the legendary ruins just examined.

Hugo divides the history of the Rhine into four periods, as noted,
and the third period, the early Middle Ages, gave rise to legend.
Understanding the historical scheme, as outlined in letter fourteen, is
important for any study of *Les Burgraves* and *La Légende des Siècles.*
There have been four distinct epochs: "l'époque antédiluvienne";
"l'époque historique ancienne," dominated by Caesar and including
the struggles between Rome and Germany; "l'époque merveilleuse,"
which saw the rise of Charlemagne; and "l'époque historique moderne," centering around conflicts between Germany and France and
dominated by Napoleon. "César, Charlemagne, et Napoléon sont les
trois énormes bornes milliaires, ou plutôt millénaires, qu'on retrouve
toujours sur son chemin" (p. 124). In the "Monographie historique du
Rhin" which Hugo did not publish, he also divides Rhine history into
four parts: "l'histoire géologique, l'histoire germaine, l'histoire

romaine, l'histoire moderne."[42] In this scheme, the Middle Ages become part of modern history, whereas in *Le Rhin,* the modern era begins with the rise of the imperial electors in the fourteenth century.[43] As a result, Hugo labels the early and high Middle Ages as legendary in *Le Rhin.* Even such historic emperors as Charlemagne, Otto I, Frederick I, and Adolph of Nassau belong to the legendary era because they are also mythical — they are given mythic qualities as time passes. "Ces hommes historiques, mêlés dans les contes aux personnages merveilleux, c'est la tradition des faits réels qui persiste sous l'encombrement des rêveries et des imaginations" (p. 118).

In a general description of historical developments in the later Middle Ages, Hugo cites the consolidation into distinct groups of a number of segments of society: princes, bishops, knights, merchants, and burgraves. He illustrates each general category by a series of allusions. For example, of the orders of chivalry, he says that "l'ordre Teutonique s'installe à Mayence, en vue de Taunus, tandis que, près de Trèves, en vue des Sept-Montagnes, les chevaliers de Rhodes s'établissent à Martinshof. De Mayence l'ordre Teutonique se ramifie jusqu'à Coblentz," and so on (p. 119). Each supporting reference is made in connection with the geography of the Rhine, and the river dominates both the choice of historical material and the form of the book.

Although discussion of the modern era is generally limited to praise of Napoleon, a later Charlemagne, Hugo's comments on the relation between the fifteenth and sixteenth centuries are of interest. A new era was ushered in by the 1500s, but the seeds of this age are to be found in the critical spirit and heretical freedom of the preceding century (p. 120). The printed book and the catapult symbolize this new epoch in thought and politics (p. 121). The emphasis differs here in comparison with *Notre-Dame de Paris* where Hugo envisions a deterioration of the medieval order on the social level and the destruction of gothic architecture by the printed book on the aesthetic level. Although he also sees the breakdown of central authority in Germany in *Le Rhin,* he accentuates the independence of spirit and the freedom of thought in the fifteenth century that would culminate with Luther.

Three medieval institutions, the empire, chivalry, and the burgraves, fascinated Hugo. His political persuasions at this time explain in part the attraction these strong figures held for him, but he also follows the emphasis of Kohlrausch, his chief historical source. Hugo tended to envision history in terms of conflicts and to admire the man who embraced an era, the hero who could resolve, even temporarily, the antithetical forces at work in a civilization. Charlemagne was such a figure, founding France and Germany under one empire, restoring civilization to the Rhine.

Pour l'histoire, c'est un grand homme comme Auguste et Sésostris; pour la fable, c'est un paladin comme Roland, un magicien comme Merlin; pour l'église, c'est un saint comme Jérôme et Pierre; pour la philosophie, c'est la civilisation même qui se personnifie, qui se fait géant tous les mille ans pour traverser quelque profond abîme, les guerres civiles, la barbarie, les révolutions, et qui s'appelle alors tantôt César, tantôt Charlemagne, tantôt Napoléon. (P. 77)

Hugo envisions control of the right bank of the Rhine by Napoleon and the later empire as a restoration of Charlemagne's realm. Letter fourteen is a protracted comparison of the two. The process of the complete deterioration of authority following the death of Charlemagne is outlined, and Hugo concludes that "ces empereurs-là sont des Titans. Ils tiennent un moment l'univers dans leurs mains, puis la mort leur écarte les doigts, et tout tombe" (p. 123).[44] The implication for Hugo's own time is that the year 1840 marks another period of breakdown in central authority along the Rhine and that new leadership is needed.

In the inevitable conflict of interests which followed the death of the strong emperor in the late Middle Ages, Hugo both admired and feared the independent burgraves, whom he called a "singular race." "Ces formidables barons du Rhin, produits robustes d'une nature âpre et farouche, nichés dans les basaltes et les bruyères, crénelés dans leur trou et servis à genoux par leurs officiers comme l'empereur, hommes de proie tenant tout ensemble de l'aigle et du hibou, puissants seulement autour d'eux mais tout-puissants autour d'eux" (p. 120). As birds of prey, the burgraves posed a threat to the Rhine because of their awe-inspiring power; they represent the forces of self-interest, a potential menace to European civilization. Chivalry developed as an institution to preserve culture. "La police par la chevalerie est un beau et curieux côté de l'histoire. L'esprit religieux, ce puissant civilisateur, défendait la chrétienté qu'il avait faite."[45] Everyone had his own interest — pope, emperor, towns included — but no one except the knight of chivalry was concerned with preserving civilization.

Conflict, the essence of drama, thus lies at the center of the history of the Rhine. The emperor, the knight, or the burgrave can be seen as the leading protagonist in each successive conflict. The ruined châteaux which have survived are silent witnesses that these past dramas always impinge on present history. "Muets témoins des temps évanouis, ils ont assisté aux actions, ils ont encadré les scènes, ils ont écouté les paroles. Ils sont là comme les coulisses éternelles du sombre drame qui, depuis dix siècles, se joue sur le Rhin" (p. 279).

6

Les Burgraves

In the preface to *Les Burgraves,* Hugo relates his drama directly to his trips along the Rhine, "longue et fantasque promenade d'antiquaire et de rêveur."[1] The burgraves and their fortresses had become real to him during his *promenades:* "Et quelles maisons que les burgs du Rhin! et quels habitants que les burgraves!" (p. 16). Repeating a comparison made in *Le Rhin,* Hugo establishes a parallel between Greek myth and the legendary Rhine; specifically, he links *Les Burgraves* with Aeschylean drama. Thessaly, like the Rhine, was sinister, and Aeschylus situated the conflict between Prometheus and the Titans on this "effrayant champ de bataille." Since history sometimes reproduces the very invention of which legend *(fable)* is comprised, the later struggle for power between Barbarossa, the Jupiter of the twelfth century, and the Burgraves, the Titans of the same era, is an analogue to the subject of Aeschylus's *Prometheus.*

Hugo is careful not to extend his analogy too far; he disclaims any intention of recreating the mythic Titans and Olympians on stage, for unlike Greek myth history has an immediacy and relevancy for the nineteenth century, a century born out of the Middle Ages (p. 14). The "reality" of historical figures gives them a compelling quality which Greek myth could not have. "Ainsi, la réalité qui éveille l'intérêt, la grandeur qui donne la poésie, la nouveauté qui passionne la foule, voilà sous quel triple aspect la lutte des burgraves et de l'empereur pouvait s'offrir à l'imagination d'un poète." There is a curious mixture of principles in this justification of the burgraves as interesting subject matter for the nineteenth century. These historical figures have a grandeur which permits the writer to create poetic drama, but they also appeal to "la foule," the public at large.

The melodrama of Hugo's theater and his array of costumes, devices, and décors of terror suggest his alliance with popular theatrical taste and his feeling that drama must be responsive to the needs of the era. Hugo "est persuadé qu'en notre temps, l'appui du peuple ne peut manquer à l'auteur dramatique dont l'oeuvre répond aux exigences profondes de son époque."[2] His consciousness of the impact *Les Burgraves* might have on the public is evidenced by his statements on the relationships between medieval history and the current political situation in Europe. From the thirteenth century, he draws the collective figure of the burgraves and their opposition to imperial authority. As for Barbarossa, his reappearance and assertion of central authority over Germany are based on Rhine legend, not on history. "Si le poète avait le droit, pour peindre l'époque, d'emprunter à l'histoire ce qu'elle enseigne, il avait également le droit d'employer, pour faire mouvoir ses personnages, ce que la légende autorise" (p. 18). The poet's prerogative in painting an earlier period is to choose those elements that have something to say to his own century. The selective process is controlled by his view of his own time, and therefore his interpretation of the past is also dependent upon his understanding of the present. Hugo justifies, implicitly, the use of medieval history and legend as a metaphor for the present and as a lesson to the nineteenth century.

For the first time Hugo intimates that he does not attempt to interpret the Middle Ages objectively or completely. The poet has the right, in painting an epoch, to borrow from history "what it teaches." In this case, the choice is not an event or even a detailed recreation of atmosphere; it is simply an antithesis: the burgraves versus the emperor. Hugo resolves the conflict between the two forces by giving superiority to the emperor. As nineteenth-century poet-statesman, he sees in the Middle Ages a metaphor for his own belief in the emperor, the alliance of France and Germany, and peace along the banks of the Rhine. He also follows Kohlrausch, his source, who had called Frederick a protector of general order in chapter nine of his history. When Hugo concludes that "le théâtre doit faire de la pensée le pain de la foule" (p. 20), his conclusion to Le Rhin, his political ambitions, and his belief — pronounced in 1849 — in a united states of Europe lie just below the surface. As Aeschylus, in recounting the fall of the Titans, once created a national work for Greece, so the poet who outlines the struggle of the burgraves "fait aujourd'hui pour l'Europe une oeuvre également nationale, dans le même sens et avec la même signification." No matter what the momentary antipathies between European nations may be, they are all indissolubly linked by a deep unity (pp. 20–21). Hugo's stance vis-à-vis the theater is hardly surprising given his long-standing sense of the vatic function of the poet and of the needs of the masses. The well-known lines of "La Fonction du poète" date from 1839, this same period, and are connected with the preface to Les Burgraves. "Peuples! écoutez le poète!/ Ecoutez le rêveur sacré!/ Dans votre nuit, sans lui complète,/ Lui seul a le front éclairé!"[3] Hugo leaves no doubt about his aims in his drama, for he has chosen a form of literary *engagement* with a firm didactic end in mind.

There are a number of other literary traditions and themes closely allied to the medieval and political elements in Les Burgraves; Hugo attempted to construct a complex ideological framework in the play.

The motif of pardon and redemption lies at the center of the play, uniting Biblical and Aeschylean precedents, and Hugo says that he wants to make the family of Job a living and complete symbol of expiation (p. 17). *Les Burgraves* brings to a conclusion the series of dramas treating the problem of pardon and fatality which begins with the double suicide of Hernani and Doña Sol despite the clemency of Charles V.[4] Fosco (Job) has attempted the crime of Cain against his brother Donato (Frederick) out of jealousy of the love between Donato and Guanhumara. As the dramatic action begins, the aged burgrave Job symbolizes remorse, Guanhumara stands for vengeance and fatality, and Barbarossa represents both providence and pardon. Resolution of the spiritual problem ends the string of catastrophes which concludes Hugo's other dramas.[5]

Hugo's use of Greek and medieval motifs in this drama is an interesting response on his part to the rediscovery of Hellenism by people such as Planche, Musset, and Sainte-Beuve, but the Greece Hugo portrays resembles the Middle Ages more than a Hellenistic ideal. "La Grèce ressemble au moyen âge — voilà la nouveauté —, mais le moyen âge ne lui cèdera pas sa place."[6] More significantly, this coupling of Greece and the Middle Ages illustrates the deepening dimensions of Hugo's world view during the 1840s. By linking Aeschylus with personal and family sin and the medieval world with national decay, Hugo indicates the inextricable bond between personal and political worlds. The prevailing mood for two-thirds of the play is dark pessimism;[7] the spell is broken by the reappearance of Frederick and pardon is given to Job at the end of the play once he has submitted to the emperor's power. Apparently, the political associations in the medieval motifs of *Les Burgraves* stem both from Hugo's keen sensitivity to personal and social evil, later sharpened under the Second Empire, and from his political ambitions. A number of tendencies in this drama were to coalesce in *La Légende des Siècles:* a concern for the large scope of history, the interpretation of the Middle Ages as an instructional model in the light of contemporary political developments, and the creation of a heroic, quasi-historical medieval period. Although *Les Burgraves* finishes on a more optimistic note than the other Romantic dramas, there is no emphasis on historical progress, as in the *Légende;* on the other hand, Barbarossa appears as a messianic figure in history who could easily be found in the later epic.

Hugo intended the form of *Les Burgraves* to reflect the diversity of its inspiration. In a passage added in the margin of the manuscript,[8] he summarizes the elements of the drama as including "l'histoire, la légende, le conte, la réalité, la nature, la famille, l'amour, des moeurs naïves, des physionomies sauvages, les princes, les soldats, les aventuriers, les rois, des patriarches ... , des chasseurs ... , des Titans." He felt himself irresistibly drawn toward this vast tableau to be painted (pp. 18–19). Such breadth of conception has caused critics to react in many different ways to the play. Jean-Bertrand Barrère's label, "this pre-Wagnerian monster," typifies the embarrassment some readers feel before such a grand synthesis on the stage.[9] Fernand Baldensperger admits that the trappings of the play are "excessively romantic" though he admires the verbal richness and verse form.[10] Olga Russell, as do many, considers the drama a work of transition in which drama is in the process of becoming epic, and, like Baldensperger, she claims that the "puissance du style éclatant et dense de l'exil" already exists here.[11] And Paul Zumthor also praises the language of the play, in contrast with the plot, noting that the picturesque imagery of the *Ballades* has become externalized in the décor.[12]

A certain ambiguity of attitude is evident in all such comments; admiration for the dense verbal texture of the play is accompanied by an uneasiness regarding the dramatic action. An examination of the role of the major monologues in relation to the *intrigue* indicates that the action of the play is, to a large extent, a symbolic fulfillment of themes stated in these important speeches. There is neither revelation of character nor the development of themes in events on stage. Particularly in parts one and two, the action is often an interlude between the "tirades fantastiques"[13] — a lament for lost greatness and for a destroyed Germany along with vituperative attacks by the burgraves against Barbarossa and by him against the rebellious lords. These long passages, tenuously connected with the main plot, dominate those sections of the play by the richness of their imagery.

The function of speech and action in *Les Burgraves* becomes clearer when one understands the relation of the double theme to the plot. Although the ideas of personal sin and public decadence are intimately related, the political motif is not as closely knit to the plot as is the theme of expiation and pardon. In the dramatic action, two generations are represented, and Guanhumara (vengeance and fatality) links the two. Fosco's supposed murder of Donato is a crime of the past, but Guanhumara's desire for revenge lives on in the present. Her plan is to save the life of the young Régina in exchange for the death of Job-Fosco at the hands of Otbert (Régina's love and Job's lost son). The plot is thwarted by Barbarossa, who stops Otbert as he is about to strike his father and who pardons Job. Little of this action occurs in the first two parts. In scenes three and four of part one, the pact is made between Otbert and Guanhumara, and the witch gives the audience the background of her hatred. In the second part, scenes two through five, Job decides to allow the marriage of Otbert to Régina, whom Guanhumara has healed by means of a potion; the senior burgrave recognizes the innocence of the young people in the face of the degradation of Hatto and the other lords. Part three is entirely devoted to the climactic action of the plot, and consequently the characters emerge from the shadows of the cave beneath the fortress in an atmosphere of sorcery, potions, and poison. This could well be the plot of an earlier melodrama, like *Angelo* or *Lucrèce Borgia*. Two additional events are of significance in the play: the arrival of the mendicant in act one and his unmasking as Barbarossa in act two. These are related directly to the political theme of disarray in Germany and the need for another strong emperor, but they also serve as dramatic peaks for the poetic statements of the political theme.

Hugo's use of so many uninterrupted monologues and sustained passages of poetry in parts one and two of this play as a means of presenting his political ideas contrasts with the soliloquies in his earlier dramas, which usually reveal conflict in a principal character. The most striking example would be, once again, the speech of Don Carlos at the tomb of Charlemagne in *Hernani* (act IV, scene 2). Earlier in the play, Doña Sol has characterized Don Carlos as a "mauvais roi" (act III, scene 6), and his treatment of her contrasts with his subsequent behavior; he becomes a benevolent, responsible emperor. The monologue does indeed convey both Hugo's understanding of the emperor's role as well as his idealization of Charlemagne; dramatically it informs us both of the change in the king's character and of his momentary conflict when he is uncertain whether he will become emperor. "— L'empereur! l'empereur! être empereur! — O rage,/ Ne pas l'être! — et sentir son coeur plein de courage! — Qu'il fut heureux celui qui dort dans ce tombeau!/ Qu'il fut grand! De son temps c'était encor plus beau."[14]

In the long speeches of *Les Burgraves* the alexandrine particularly suited Hugo's expansive poetic powers, and *remplissage* (amplification of a specific kind) is a basic element of his versification, according to Michel Butor.[15] A major means of achieving *remplissage* is by the accompanying voice of another character who supplies the missing syllables, acting as a reinforcement or decoration to the first speaker. Other devices include gestures, silences, and music which interrupt the poetic flow at significant moments.[16] Butor also stresses the importance of the aside, for as a result of this logic of versification, the characters speak in verse, not among themselves, but for us, the audience.[17]

The speech of Job which opens part three of *Les Burgraves* illustrates these techniques of versification. Alone on stage, Job discloses his reluctant capitulation to the power of Barbarossa and his personal sense of guilt for past crime. This soliloquy serves the usual function of revealing the inner conflict of the character. It also becomes a prelude to the unraveling of the plot. Punctuated by gestures and silences, the speech is accompanied by a voice from the shadows which addresses Job as "Caïn." At its weakest, the poetry is manipulated for purposes of rhyme.

> Quoi! c'est le comte Job! quoi! c'est moi qui succombe! . . .
> Silence, orgueil! tais-toi du moins dans cette tombe!
>   (Il promène ses regards autour de lui.)
> C'est ici, sous ces murs qu'on dirait palpitants,
> Qu'en une nuit pareille . . . Oh! voilà bien longtemps,
> Et c'est toujours hier! Horreur! . . .
>
> (pp. 108–9)

At the points of more intense emotion, however, the alexandrines achieve a grandeur by their succession of images. For instance, the meeting of Job and the Emperor reunites the last survivors of a world which has been submerged. "— L'empereur! — Nous étions l'un pour l'autre un fantôme;/ Et nous nous regardions d'un oeil presque ébloui!/ Comme les deux géants d'un monde évanoui!"

The principal speeches of parts one and two, though displaying these same strengths and weaknesses of versification, present the political theme. Specifically, they provide antithetical points of view toward the state of affairs along the Rhine; the burgraves speak out in favor of their independence while the Emperor laments political disunity. The prolixity of the early sections of the play, though related to Hugo's use of the alexandrine, derives from his conscious attempt to impress his view of the Rhine question upon the theater audience by means of his own poetic rhetoric. Before the audience hears Magnus and Job, spokesmen for the burgraves, and the Emperor, the slaves of the *burg* set the verbal tone of part one. In a long expository scene, the slaves reply to one another in a counterpoint of alexandrines, providing information about the characters in the play and the legendary background of Job and Barbarossa. The stories that Barbarossa lived on after his supposed death and would reappear, the glorification of the burgraves' wars, and the references to the independent fortresses are all directly related to *Le Rhin*.[18] "C'étaient des guerres de géants!/ Les burgraves entre eux se prêtaient tous main-forte" (p. 44).

With the appearance of Hatto and the dissolute younger generation ("Jadis on guerroyait, maintenant on s'amuse./ Jadis c'était la force, à présent c'est la ruse"), in scene 6 Magnus laments the decayed honor of the burgraves and attacks Barbarossa. The imagery combines the concrete and the visionary which are to characterize the best of the poetry after exile. The vituperative tone of *Les Châtiments* is also evident. The general theme, "O souvenirs! ô temps! tout s'est évanoui!," is reinforced by imagery of darkness and light. The following sustained metaphor exemplifies the interplay of imagery and theme; the glistening steel of the burgraves' pledge of honor has been replaced by the tinsel and phoney silk of new fashion.

> Jadis il en était
> Des serments qu'on faisait dans la vieille Allemagne
> Comme de nos habits de guerre et de campagne;
> Ils étaient en acier. — J'y songe avec orgueil. —
> C'était chose solide et reluisante à l'oeil,
> Que l'on entamait point sans lutte et sans bataille,
> A laquelle d'un homme on mesurait la taille,
> Qu'un noble avait toujours présente à son chevet,
> Et qui, même rouillée, était bonne et servait.
> . . . .
> Mais aujourd'hui la foi, l'honneur et les paroles
> Ont pris le train nouveau des modes espagnoles.
> Clinquant! soie!

(P. 66)

The tone becomes more bitter as Magnus lays blame for the destruction of the honor and the power of the burgraves on the shoulders of Barbarossa and, in turn, vows his vengeance: "Trente ans, sous ce césar qui toujours triomphait,/ L'incendie et l'exil, les fers, mille aventures,/ Les juges, les cachots, les greffiers, les tortures,/ Oui, nous avons souffert tout cela!" (pp. 68–69).

When Frederick I arrives in disguise, Job greets him with another bitter outburst, proclaiming himself "Un burgrave fameux parmi tous les burgraves" and "Ce vieux titan du Rhin, Job l'excommunié." Here is Prometheus in splendid, horrid isolation: "Isolé, foudroyé, reprouvé, mais resté/ Debout dans sa montagne et dans sa volonté" (p. 74). There is something admirable in this independence of spirit, and after Hugo's exile, a change of emphasis transforms Job into Welf, "un spectre en liberté songeant au fond des nuits."

Although Hugo conceived the history of the Rhine in terms of physical conflict, confrontation in *Les Burgraves* takes place at the verbal level. In part two, the mendicant reveals that he is Frederick I, and the conflict which then occurs between him and the burgraves is one of antithetical points of view, with Job finally opting for "une Allemagne au monde." In scene six, the threat of violence is presented entirely in terms of the *mise en scène*. When Magnus defies the emperor before Job makes his sudden speech of submission, the emperor is surrounded by a circle of burgraves, a line of soldiers, three deep and heavily armed appears, and the banner of the *burg* waves above the soldiers (p. 102). The conflict is never interiorized; the representative characters make pronouncements about history on a large scale and about their symbolic roles within the empire. The succession of images and historical references compresses several centuries into one general impression.[19] The speeches of the emperor combine concrete detail (drawn from history, in this case) and suggestive metaphor.

> Allemagne, ô patrie!
> Que tes fils sont déchus! et de quels coups meurtrie,
> Après ce long exil, je te retrouve, hélas!
> Ils ont tué Philippe, et chassé Ladislas,
> Empoisonné Heinrich! Ils ont, d'un front tranquille
> Vendu Coeur-de-Lion comme ils vendraient Achille!
> O chute affreuse et sombre! abaissement profond!
> Plus d'unité. Les noeuds des Etats se défont.
>
> (P. 77)

Frederick does not castigate the older burgraves, members of his own generation, but he does attack the corrupt brigands who now pillage the Rhine, calling them *chacals* and *orfraies.*

The tribute Job pays to Barbarossa when he submits to him summarizes the political theme of the play. "Vous êtes nécessaire aux nations frappées;/ Vous seul! Sans vous l'Etat touche aux derniers moments" (p. 104). Hugo's Bonapartism of 1843 is also at the heart of Job's words. Such verbalizing of political ideas makes *Les Burgraves* a static drama; its failure on the stage suggests that Hugo had not found the proper vehicle for his vision of the past. Parts one and two of the play can be envisaged as a series of tableaux, not unlike a Wagnerian opera, in which the arias of the mythic heroes correspond to the densely imaged monologues of Magnus, Job, or Frederick Barbarossa. Like *Notre-Dame de Paris, Les Burgraves* illustrates Hugo's ambivalent attitude toward the Middle Ages, but by the 1840s he articulated more sharply the parallels he saw between the past and the political and social injustice of the present.

7

The Poet in Exile

The role of medieval motif for Hugo's poetic inspiration changed considerably after 1843. The death of Léopoldine, the affair with Léonie Biard, the responsibilities of peer and deputy, and events leading to his exile all but silenced Hugo as a published voice before the appearance of *Histoire d'un crime, Napoléon-le-petit,* and *Les Châtiments.* Privately, of course, he was at work on *Les Misères* and some of the poems of *Les Contemplations,* and between 1846 and 1850, he wrote "Le Mariage de Roland" and "Aymerillot" which would eventually appear in the medieval section of *La Légende des Siècles.* Exile crystallized Hugo's epic vision, and during the years 1856 to 1859 when he was preparing the first series of the *Légende,* he again devoted his attention to the Middle Ages, writing a number of poems with medieval motifs for his epic cycle. These years mark his final concentration on the medieval period; only a few later additions to the *Légende* contain medieval narrative patterns.

The scattered images and allusions to the Middle Ages in the writings of the exile years place both Hugo's attitude toward his role as a poet in exile and his mature view of history in a unique perspective. Even in *Napoléon-le-petit,* occasional references to medieval civilization mark a significant shift in Hugo's view of the period. The Middle Ages remain a political metaphor, but medieval institutions now represent the major obstacles to historical progress in the modern period. Louis-Napoléon is described as "un homme d'un autre temps" and therefore out-of-step with the nineteenth century. "Il y a en lui du moyen âge et du bas-empire."[1] There have been four material obstacles to the realization of the democratic ideal: "l'armée permanente, l'administration centralisée, le clergé fonctionnaire, la magistrature inamovible."[2] Napoléon III embodies the resistance to the inevitable forces within history at work in 1848 to do away with these institutions. History is always at work creating the new out of the old. "Peu à peu la ruine se prépare."[3] At this moment of decay, a strong revolutionary figure is needed to finish the destructive processes of history and to create the new order. The year 1848 was a critical moment when enlightened leadership was needed. "La vieille Europe féodale, monarchique et papale, replâtrée si fatalement pour la France en 1815, chancela. Mais Danton manquait. L'écroulement n'eut pas lieu."[4]

Hugo's scathing attacks on the French political leadership and his overt use of literature as a vehicle for these attacks coincide with his complete identification with Dante, that other exiled poet. The comparison between the two figures was not just a product of Hugo's imagination, however. In 1852 Gautier commented that the sale of the household belongings of the Hugo family was "un spectacle navrant," referring to Hugo as "le plus grand poète de la France, maintenant en exil comme Dante, et qui apprend par expérience combien il est douloureusement vrai du vieux gibelin: Il est dur de monter par l'escalier d'autrui."[5] The analogy between Hugo and Dante was widespread enough that the performance of Bornier's drama *Dante et Béatrice* was canceled by Napoléon III for fear that the play might be interpreted in the light of recent political events.[6]

Hugo's literary use of the figure of Dante becomes increasingly complex because Hugo makes the medieval poet symbolic of his own role in the literary and political worlds of the nineteenth century. Dante is no longer linked with Virgil; rather, he is coupled with Juvenal to represent Hugo as satirist and polemicist against the Second Empire. In the well-known ninth stanza of "Nox," introductory poem to *Les Châtiments,* Hugo places himself directly behind a succession of indignant poets represented by Juvenal and Dante.

> Toi qu'aimait Juvénal gonflé de lave ardente,
> Toi dont la clarté luit dans l'oeil fixe de Dante,
> Muse Indignation, viens, dressons maintenant,
> Dressons sur cette empire heureux et rayonnant,
> Et sur cette victoire au tonnerre échappée,
> Assez de piloris pour faire une épopée.[7]

This same association is stressed later in *William Shakespeare.* "Ce que Juvénal fait pour la Rome des césars, Dante le fait pour la Rome des papes; mais Dante est justicier à un degré plus redoutable que Juvénal; Juvénal fustige avec des lanières, Dante fouette avec des flammes; Juvénal condamne, Dante damne." Not only the State but the Church, as chief supporter of Napoleon's illegal rule, shares in Hugo's wrath. He notes that Rabelais followed Dante chronologically and suggests that each represents a different reaction against the Church. "Dante et Rabelais arrivent de l'école des cordeliers, comme plus tard Voltaire des jésuites; Dante le deuil, Rabelais la parodie, Voltaire l'ironie; cela sort de l'église contre l'église."[8]

Hugo often paired Dante with other poets, depending upon what symbolic role he wished him to play. For example, in *La Pitié suprême* Dante and Isaiah are the voices of conscience, of condemnation and of truth.[9] Dante, the misunderstood Florentine, is a tragic figure when juxtaposed to Petrarch, a happy poet understood in his own time. "Pétrarque est une lumière de son temps, et c'est une belle chose qu'une lumière qui vient de l'amour."[10] But Hugo prefers the staff of the wandering Dante to the purple robe of the laureate. "Il manque à Pétrarque cet on ne sait quoi de tragique qui ajoute à la grandeur des poètes une cime noire, et qui a toujours marqué le plus haut sommet du génie. Il lui manque l'insulte, le deuil, l'affront, la persécution. Dans la gloire Pétrarque est dépassé par Dante, et le triomphe par l'exil."[11]

Hugo's sympathies for the cause of a unified, free Italy were well-known during his exile, and in his mind Dante became the symbol of Italy and of the inevitable triumph of justice. When the city of Florence invited Hugo to attend the celebration of the six-hundredth anniversary of Dante's birth in 1865,[12] Hugo replied: "Comme lui, elle est vaillante, pensive, altière, magnanime, propre au combat, propre à l'idée. Comme lui, elle amalgame, dans une synthèse profonde, la poésie et la philosophie."[13] Dante gave birth to the idea that right and justice had to prevail, an idea that bloomed only in the nineteenth century. "Les rêves des grands hommes sont les gestations de l'avenir. Les penseurs songent conformément à ce que doit être."[14]

As a natural extension of his admiration for Dante the exile and visionary, Hugo includes him in the list of *génies* in *William Shakespeare,* but he always emphasizes the dark side of Dante's work. Repeating the imagery of "Après une lecture de Dante," Hugo magnifies the "spirale aux bords douteux" until it becomes the *Inferno* itself, "ce poème gouffre."

> Dante tord toute l'ombre et toute la clarté dans une spirale monstrueuse. Cela descend, puis cela monte. Architecture inouïe. Au seuil est la brume sacrée. En travers de l'entrée est étendu le cadavre de l'espérance. Tout ce qu'on aperçoit au delà est nuit. L'immense angoisse sanglote confusément dans l'invisible. On se penche sur ce poëme gouffre; est-ce un cratère? . . . c'est l'enfer. Ceci n'est plus le milieu humain. On est dans le précipice inconnu.[15]

The *Comedy* is an apocalypse, a vision, which both descends and ascends. This double action, which Hugo sees in Shakespeare as well, characterizes his own works.[16] The world of both Dante and Shakespeare is full of shadows: "Shakespeare, autant que Dante, laisse entrevoir l'horizon crépusculaire de la conjecture. Dans l'un comme dans l'autre il y a le possible, cette fenêtre du rêve ouverte sur le réel."[17] Hugo suggests that the dream world of the two authors opens another dimension of reality, casting a different light on the world of ordinary appearances.

Beyond Dante, whose genius he admired so much, there was little else in the Middle Ages to attract the anti-authoritarian and anticlerical Hugo of the exile years. This general disaffection for the Middle Ages is most clearly paralleled by the historian Michelet's attitude;[18] his distaste for the medieval period, partly the result of an earlier anti-clericalism, antedates the coup of Napoléon III. Michelet's philosophy of history, particularly his belief in the progressive liberation of man, glorifies the Renaissance and the revolutionary periods in contrast to the Middle Ages.[19] In his introduction to the seventh volume of the *Histoire de France* Michelet juxtaposes the Middle Ages and the Renaissance: "L'état bizarre et monstrueux, prodigieusement artificiel, qui fut celui du moyen âge, n'a d'argument en sa faveur que son extrême durée, sa résistance obstinée au retour de la nature."[20] Feudalism, the Church, gothic art, and medieval science all bear the brunt of Michelet's attack. For Michelet medieval culture was dead after the twelfth century.[21]

Once the popular craze for the Middle Ages had died down, Michelet could speak of his earlier writing about the gothic in volume two of his history as blindly enthusiastic. "Mon trop aveugle enthousiasme s'explique par un mot; nous devinions, et nous avions la fièvre de la devination."[22] The government and the clergy promoted the glorification of the gothic by their restoration of medieval edifices, but this campaign was part of a political plan to maintain bourgeois-Catholic power. Now, says Michelet, exercising the new art of historical criticism, scientific study of gothic architecture indicates that this enthusiasm to save the monuments of France is misplaced. Only very late gothic churches were carefully constructed. In fact, gothic churches were fragile edifices and what the nineteenth century knows as gothic is largely a patched-up restoration.[23]

Having been a member of the Comité des Arts et Monuments, Hugo never went so far as to attack gothic architecture. And, although both he and Michelet could condemn medieval institutions and the repression of the masses within the feudal system, they could admire the heroic figures who symbolized the possibility of progress in an otherwise bleak period.[24] Aside from *La Légende des Siècles,* which indicates Hugo's mature historical vision, his other occasional statements and references are as damning as Michelet's introduction to the *Renaissance.* They are the logical extension of the ambivalence of the "negative medievalism" which he had already exhibited in the early 1830s.

Several allusions to the Middle Ages in *Les Misérables* enhance this portrayal of innate human heroism and love, the social milieu of the July Revolution, and the atmosphere of nineteenth-century Paris. Since the accumulation of descriptive details suggests historical authenticity, Hugo alludes from time to time to the medieval Paris he had studied for *Notre-Dame de Paris*. But for Hugo, developing the themes of *Les Misérables*, this Paris of the 1830s becomes the social hell of humanity, symbolized by Jean Valjean's struggle in the sewers — "le vieux cloaque gothique."[25]

Marius, like Hugo, experiences a period of Bonapartism; he thinks of Napoleon as following in the steps of Charlemagne. "Il [Napoléon] fut le prodigieux architecte d'un écroulement, le continuateur de Charlemagne, de Louis XI, de Henri IV, de Richelieu, de Louis XIV et du comité de salut public."[26] Although this phase in Marius's evolution is significant, the political focus of the novel is on the democratic revolutionaries: "farouches et effrayants pour le bien." In opposition to the revolutionaries, Hugo sees all those who would uphold the status quo as refined dandies. These men "insistent doucement pour le maintien et la conservation du passé, du moyen-âge, du droit divin, du fanatisme, de l'ignorance, de l'esclavage, de la peine de mort, de la guerre, glorifiant à demi-voix et avec politesse le sabre, le bûcher et l'échafaud. Quant à nous, si nous étions forcés à l'option entre les barbares de la civilisation et les civilisés de la barbarie, nous choisirions les barbares."[27] Nothing could be more explicit; the term medieval stands for all the monarchical, religious, and social evils inherited by the generation of 1830 — social evils that only a revolution could eliminate. The movement of 1789 succeeded, at least, in destroying absolutism. "Grâce à la révolution, les conditions sociales sont changées. Les maladies féodales et monarchiques ne sont plus dans notre sang. Il n'y a plus de Moyen Age dans notre constitution."[28]

The effect of Hugo's political and religious position on his interpretation of the medeval mind is most striking in *Promontorium somnii* which, again, is an extension of earlier attitudes present in *La Préface de Cromwell* and *Le Rhin*. The capacity of medieval man to animate his world, to populate it with unreal creatures, is called "la chimère gothique." "Les diverses théogonies sont, sans exception, idolâtrie par un côté et philosophie par l'autre. Toute leur philosophie, qui contient leur vérité, peut se résumer par le mot Religion; et toute leur idolâtrie, qui contient leur politique, peut se résumer par le mot Chimérisme."[29] This animating fancy, a compensation for lack of religious and political freedom, functioned on various levels, ranging from superstition to belief in legend.

Initially, "les apparences crépusculaires abondent. Les superstitions prennent corps. La diablerie commence."[30] The physical world is animated and, then, populated with fantastic creatures such as *psylles, nages, alungles,* and *vampires*. Animals are given human qualities as man himself becomes bestial. "La bête, dont il se rapproche, fait un pas de son côté; elle prend quelque chose d'humain qui inquiète. Ce loup est le sire Isengrin, ce hibou est le docteur Sapiens."[31] Medieval Christian mythology is a gothic phantasmagoria. "Le Dieu morcelé de l'antiquité est encore le seul que puisse comprendre le moyen-âge. Le Christ a fait à peine diversion au fétichisme. Un paganisme chrétien pullule sur l'Evangile."[32] Finally, "gothic legend" can be said to be the most intriguing product of the medieval imagination, for it transforms the world of normal appearances. "Aucun [monde] ne dépasse la légende gothique. En haut le mirage, en bas le vertige. . . . C'est la géographie du cauchemar."[33]

Hugo concludes that this sinister dream world existed in the Middle Ages as a direct result of feudalism. "Hélas, le moyen-âge est lugubre. Ce pauvre paysan féodal ne lui marchandez pas son rêve. C'est à peu près tout ce qu'il possède. Son champ n'est pas à lui, son toit n'est pas à lui. Le seigneur a la carcasse, le prêtre a l'âme. Le serf végète entre eux deux, une moitié dans un enfer, une moitié dans l'autre."[34] In describing the medieval mind as infantile and in suggesting that feudal suppression lay behind its fantastic world, Hugo parallels Michelet's *La Sorcière*, which was published at the beginning of 1863. (Hugo's manuscript is dated as being written in December of that year.) Michelet describes the despair of the Middle Ages in which the individual had no worth whatsoever, indicating that the interest of women in imaginary creatures was a form of escapism and suggests the absence of God for the medieval mind led to the acceptance of the reality of Satan. Behind this despair Michelet sees the institution of feudalism. "L'incertitude de la condition, la pente horriblement glissante par laquelle l'homme libre devient *vassal*, — le vassal *serviteur*, — et le serviteur *serf*, c'est la terreur du moyen âge et le fonds de son désespoir."[35]

Many of the references in the discussion of the "chimère gothique" in *Promontorium somnii* parallel volume two of François-Victor Hugo's translation of Shakespeare.[36] Evidently, Hugo attributed all that was fantastic in Shakespeare to the heritage from the Middle Ages because in *William Shakespeare* he claims that "ces deux génies, Homère et Shakespeare, ferment les deux premières portes de la barbarie, la porte antique et la porte gothique."[37] A similar point of view exists in François-Victor's introduction to *Le Songe d'une nuit d'été* and *La Tempête*. The supernatural creatures of the two plays are seen as the products of a sixteenth-century imagination, which differs little from the "chimère gothique." Shakespeare's audience accepted these beings as a part of reality. "Tous ces êtres, relégués aujourd'hui dans la fantaisie, prenaient place alors dans la réalité. Ils vivaient, non pas seulement de la vie de l'art, mais de la vie de la nature."[38] In indicating ways in which humanity has attempted to combat its suppression, François-Victor concludes that "la sorcellerie était l'insurrection sacrilège de toutes les misères contre la loi humaine, de toutes les douleurs contre la loi divine. Elle était la franc-maçonnerie suprême du désespoir."[39]

An excellent illustration of Hugo's increasingly severe attitude toward the Middle Ages is the subtle evolution of the meaning of the term *gothique* in his poetry and prose.[40] In the *Odes,* Hugo speaks of the colorful "temps gothiques" and also uses the adjective as a general architectural term, but in *Notre-Dame de Paris* he is concerned with accurate description and works out a theory of the rise of gothic architecture. Occasionally in his poetry he also places the architectural term in a new context for poetic effect.[41] After exile, however, *gothique* becomes a synonym for *médiéval* and often assumes pejorative overtones. The phrases "le vieux cloaque gothique" and "la porte gothique [de la barbarie]" from *Les Misérables* and *William Shakespeare* respectively illustrate that distaste for medieval institutions lies behind Hugo's use of the word *gothique* in many nonarchitectural contexts. Similarly, in *L'Homme qui rit,* he refers to "législation gothique" or "gothiques prisons."[42] Or in *Dieu,* speaking specifically in a religious context, he maintains the architectural connotations of the word but extends his negative vision of medieval institutions into the realm of art. "Dieu gothique, irritable, intolérant, tueur,/ Noir vitrail effrayant qu'empourpre la lueur/ Du bûcher qui flamboie et pétille derrière . . ."[43] By the end of his career, Hugo made the adjective *gothique* a weapon of specific attack in criticizing his own society. Thus, in attacking clerical control of French education, he could lash out against "le traînement du syllabus gothique."[44]

Attraction for the figure of Dante and repugnance for the institutionalized life of the Middle Ages affect Hugo's conception of the form of "La Vision de Dante," a poem which illustrates many aspects of the medievalism of his exile years. Originally designated to be the eighth book of *Les Châtiments,* the poem was published in the "série complémentaire" of *La Légende des Siècles* in 1883, though it was written in 1853. Its subject matter separates it from the other "medieval" poems of the *Légende* because it is essentially a condemnation of suppression and cruelty in France and Italy under the aegis of the Pope and the Austrian and French governments.

In attacking those who deny human freedom, Hugo adopts the form of the apocalyptic vision which he considers appropriate in part because it is medieval. His empathy with Dante is so complete that he can attribute his own vision to the Italian poet. Dante-Hugo envisions the damnation of Pope Pious IX, Napoléon III, Frederick II, and Nicholas I; the implied precedents from the Italian Middle Ages give added authority to this latter-day *Inferno.* Consequently, there is a change in the method by which Hugo portrays the parallels he claims exist between the negative aspects of his era and those of the Middle Ages.

In *Les Burgraves,* he had interpreted the Middle Ages in the light of the nineteenth century. Here, he portrays his own century in a literary form, the vision, which is supposedly medieval. The historical parallels between the nineteenth century and the era of Dante are implied.

Maurice Lange has stated bluntly that there is no connection between Hugo's work and the *Divine Comedy.*[45] He has identified the sources of the apocalyptic allusions as Revelation, Job, Ezekiel, and Isaiah and indicates that the actual literary precedent for both *Les Châtiments* and "La Vision de Dante" is *Les Tragiques* of d'Aubigné. The historical allusions are taken from the *mémoires* of General Pepe in his *Histoire des révolutions et des guerres d'Italie en 1847, 1848 et 1849.* Yet, the "Vision" epitomizes the Dante-Juvenal aspect of Hugo's role as poet in exile, and this analogy in turn affects the way he portrays history.

In the poem there is a sharp contrast between sections one through five and six through seventeen. The initial lines introduce the vision and indicate its nature and setting. The second part is comprised of a succession of groups: the suffering masses, the armies, captains, judges, rulers, and the Pope, who are interrogated by the angel Justice; it concludes with the judgment and condemnation of the Pope. The division between these two parts of the poem is accentuated by the rhythm. The slow movement of the first lines reflects the somber vision. "— Pas un vent, pas un bruit,/ Pas un souffle; la mort, la nuit; nulle rencontre;/ Rien, pas même une chute affreuse ne se montre."[46] The pace quickens when the archangel calls forth the sinners and the vast abyss of shadows begins to take on life.

> C'était comme un point noir, puis comme une fumée,
> Puis comme la poussière où s'avance une armée,
> Puis comme une île d'ombre au sein des nuits flottant,
> Et cet amas sinistre et lourd, vers nous montant,
> Triste, livide, énorme, ayant un air de rage,
> Venait et grandissait, poussé d'un vent d'orage.
>
> (P. 664)

Extending Dante's original "vision," the poet penetrates a formless void, not a geometric hell; with a long series of qualifiers he creates an almost palpable void and expands the central image of *l'ombre:* "l'ombre hideuse, ignorée, insondable,/ De l'invisible Rien vision formidable,/ Sans forme, sans contour, sans plancher, sans plafond,/ Où dans l'obscurité l'obscurité se fond" (p. 661). The only source of light is behind the seven angels, and this emanation heightens the infinitude of the abyss. "L'abîme obscur, hagard, funèbre, illimité,/ Semblait plein de terreur devant cette lumière" (p. 662). Thus, it is Hugo-Dante who can proceed beyond the limits of time and give form to the formless. It was only a small advance for Hugo to move from this particular damnation of his contemporaries to a broader epic vision, embracing all of time. *La Légende des Siècles,* though a series of poems, is placed in the framework of a vision, but Hugo sees the vision himself, not through the persona of Dante. "J'eus un rêve: le mur des siècles m'apparut." "Cette vision sombre, abrégé noir du monde,/ Allait s'évanouir dans une aube profonde,/ Et, commencée en nuit, finissait en lueur."[47]

La Légende des Siècles

Charles Baudelaire paid tribute to the originality of Hugo's epic when he said of *La Légende des Siècles* that "Victor Hugo a créé le seul poème épique qui pût être créé par un homme de son temps pour les lecteurs de son temps."[1] Both the "primary" and "secondary" epic forms[2] had aroused interest earlier in the period. The neo-classical epic had retained its popularity and the desire to write a long, narrative poem was strong among the Romantics, particularly Lamartine. As Herbert J. Hunt has indicated, writers such as Ballanche, Quinet, and Soumet also tried to put their metaphysical systems into epic form.[3]

On the other hand, Romanticism had brought "popular" poetry (or the "primary" epic) to the attention of the public. When the ideas of Herder were being disseminated in France, Abel Hugo edited and translated the *Romancero*. The Baron von Eckstein lectured on eastern and western epic poetry at the Société des Bonnes Lettres and published extracts of "popular" poetry in the *Annales* and the *Catholique*. Hugo himself repeats Romantic theory about the "primary" epic as late as the 1860s when he comments that "ces puissantes légendes épiques, testaments des âges, tatouages imprimés par les races sur l'histoire, n'ont pas d'autre unité que l'unité même du peuple. Le collectif et le successif, en se combinant, font un. *Turba fit mens.*"[4] The orginal scheme for the *Légende,* a series of "petites épopées," also reveals Hugo's interest in popular poetry. The two earliest medieval poems in the work, "Le Mariage de Roland" and "Aymerillot," are based on Jubinal's faulty popularization of contemporary scholarship on the *chanson de geste*, but they indicate that Hugo's original intention was to create a number of short narrative poems with a basis in history.[5]

Eventually, Hugo extended the meaning of the term epic far beyond its narrow, generic definition. The 1859 preface indicates that the *Légende* is epic because of the magnitude and scope of its conception — just as *Notre-Dame de Paris* and *Les Burgraves* were characterized by epic dimensions. Hugo says that his ambition was "exprimer l'humanité dans une espèce d'oeuvre cyclique; la peindre successivement et simultanément sous tous ces aspects."[6] Hugo is concerned less with an accurate protrayal of the historical details of each successive century than with the collective movement of humanity. Although there is a plethora of historical detail in the *Légende,* Hugo is not concerned with accuracy; he mixes legend and history for a special local color. The legendary was as valid as historical fact in a literary reconstruction of an era.

In the *Légende,* the most important poems (those pointing to man's progress, particularly "Le Satyre," "Pleine mer," and "Plein ciel") bypass the restrictive limits of time by their mythic and visionary qualities. Published in the 1859 *recueil,* these poems are written more in the vein of *La Fin de Satan* and *Dieu.* They are doors permitting us to pass from one historical period to another, ending with an apocalyptic future.[7] The *Légende* is only the first work of a proposed trilogy so that the epic scope of Hugo's creative ambitions is not restricted by recorded history, and the past is of less importance than the future.

> C'est l'avenir, — du moins tel qu'on le voit en songe, —
> Quand le monde atteindra son but, quand les instants,
> Les jours, les mois, les ans, auront rempli le temps.
> . . . .
> Le beau Progrès vermeil, l'oeil sur l'azur fixé,
> Marche, et tout en marchant dévore le passé.[8]

Hugo shared with others of his century the obsession with discovering the laws of historical development.[9] But much of this interest in finding the end of history stemmed from the personal conviction that the future must justify his own political choices. In 1855, he wrote about this end in a letter. "Je ne suis pas pressé, moi, car je suis beaucoup plus occupé du lendemain que de l'aujourd'hui. Le lendemain devra être formidable, destructeur, réparateur et toujours juste."[10] In working out his belief in both social and cosmic progress, Hugo formulated a vision of history, evident in his poetry, but never explicitly stated as a philosophy of history.

Again, there are striking parallels between Michelet and Hugo. Both interpreted history as the progress of man toward liberty, although not as a continuous movement without setbacks. Both saw in history a sequence of symbolic actions as "l'humanité se crée." And both recognized that the nature of human progress derived from the double nature of man, "homo duplex" with his capacity for good and evil. Michelet had absorbed Vico and the German historians, but in the *Légende,* belief in progress is expressed through images, particularly of ascent into light, and by the theme of love. Nevertheless, the orientation of the epic is toward the metaphysical beliefs of the exile years, not toward nineteenth-century historicism.[11]

> L'air est plein de senteurs douces,
> Un ensemencement de fleurs couvre les mousses,
> L'homme est ombre; on ne peut guère dire pourquoi

Nous sommes sur la terre. Et bien, je le dis, moi,
C'est pour aimer. . . .[12]

Of revolutions, however, Hugo has little to say, for love is the liberating force of the spirit.[13] "Les révolutions, archanges de clarté,/ N'ont mis que la moitié de l'homme en liberté!/ L'autre est encore aux fers, et c'est la plus divine."[14]

This idea of progress affects both the form of the work and the interpretation of history; it displaces the largely anecdotal quality of the original conception.[15] History is also a series of symbolic actions which have either promoted or hindered human progress. Few qualifications or refinements of historical vision are possible in this "grand ensemble blanc-noir du monde."[16] The characters in the drama of recorded history are as symbolic as those of *Les Burgraves*. If Hugo shows any concern for detailed historical interpretation, it is to illustrate the pattern of tyranny and oppression against which man must fight. A number of symbolic tyrants and heroes thus emerge, and the implications of their struggles would have been clear to the reader living under the rule of Napoléon III. Charles Baudouin has seen the theme of the hero and the villain in terms of the archetypal myth of the combat between man and a monster or dragon: "l'Homme, qui se dresse contre *les rois* et *les dieux,* ses maîtres de toujours, à la manière du héros provoquant le monstre."[17]

In the spectrum of history, Hugo was still drawn toward the European Middle Ages, toward the era of *chevaliers* and usurping tyrants, heroes and monster figures. The organization of the first series of poems of the *Légende* (1859) indicates how completely the opposition between progress and political oppression dominates Hugo's interpretation of the medeval period. After the key poem "Conscience," symbolizing the remorse of fallen man in the section entitled "D'Eve à Jésus," we pass quickly from Rome and Islam to the Middle Ages, which provide the setting for more poems than any other era. This series ("Le Cycle héroïque chrétien," "Les Chevaliers errants," "Les Trônes d'Orient," "L'Italie — Ratbert") characterizes the repression that results from rule by the unjust. There is a succession of malicious rulers such as the Spanish kings of "Le Jour des Rois," the "infants d'Asturie," Joss and Zéno of "Eviradnus," Ratbert, and Gaïffer-Jorge. Hugo even defends himself on this point in the preface. He says that the disproportionate thematic emphasis on oppression in the medieval section of *La Légende des Siècles* will be counterbalanced by the completed poem, with its movement toward freedom. The sections added in 1877, "Après les Dieux, les Rois," "Avertissements et Châtiments," and "Le Cycle pyrénéen," reinforce this picture of an age of oppression; fixed republicanism and opposition to the rule of Napoléon III are the determining factors in this pessimistic portrayal of the Middle Ages.

In the collection of 1859, the series describing the despotic and corrupt Ratbert is followed immediately by "Le Satyre," the Renaissance myth which is the pivotal poem of the work. The contrast between the two eras appears complete; the Middle Ages become "la prison qu'on brise."[18] In both *Notre-Dame de Paris* and *Le Rhin,* Hugo had juxtaposed the fifteenth and sixteenth centuries, describing the Renaissance as a revolution of the human spirit, illustrated best by the influence of the printed word. The "Satyre" embodies these opinions in his Promethean defiance of the gods, and his transformation into Pan as he sings of man's slow ascent toward freedom. This mythic pattern indicates the importance Hugo attached to the Renaissance as does the fact that he defined the era in terms of the creativity of the human spirit.[19] The myth also describes Hugo's all-embracing poetic experience and consequently takes precedence over the narratives of the monster kings of the Middle Ages. The short poem "L'Hydre" of the second series suggests the mythic pattern of the epic's medieval poems. A knight approaches the monster who asks why he has come. "Est-ce pour moi, réponds, ou pour le roi Ramire?/ — C'est pour le monstre. — Alors, c'est pour le roi, beau sir,/ Et l'hydre, reployant ses noeuds, se recoucha" (p. 86).

Another facet to Hugo's portrayal of the Middle Ages is the extension of his interest in chivalry.[20] Although darkness and despotism mark the medieval world, the knight represents the light of progress — the individual with colossal strength and penetrating vision who rises above his century, if only for a brief period. "C'est une période de ténèbres où ne surgit ici ou là, comme une trouée de jour, qu'un être de fraîcheur et de force en qui s'épanouit un printemps d'héroïsme."[21]

As I have already indicated,[22] "La terre a vu jadis errer des paladins," the introductory poem to the cycle "Les Chevaliers errants," is one of the most effective presentations of the knight.

> La terre a vu jadis errer des paladins;
> Ils flamboyaient ainsi que des éclairs soudains,
> Puis s'évanouissaient, laissant sur les visages
> La crainte, et la lueur de leurs brusques passages;
> Ils étaient, dans des temps d'oppression, de deuil,
> De honte, où l'infamie étalait son orgueil,
> Les spectres de l'honneur, du droit, de la justice.
>
> (P. 211)

The imagery conveys the great gulf separating these individuals from the masses. The knights are a sudden, evanescent gleam in the night, leaving behind a reflection of themselves. They inspire fear, and their bellicose nature is suggested by the adjective "brusque." Hugo calls them "éclairs soudains," an image denoting action, and "spectres" of honor, right, and justice, indicating the visionary powers of these figures who remind a depraved era of vanished moral good.

Subsequent lines reinforce these images, but in the final stanzas the chivalric quest is conveyed by geographical, historical, and legendary allusions denoting voyage. Dürer's knight from the Rhine and the mysterious, shadowy *paladin* supersede the imagery of light which begins the poem. "O les noirs chevaucheurs! ô les marcheurs sans trêve!"

> Partout où surgissait leur ombre colossale,
> On sentait la terreur des pays inconnus;
> Celui-ci vient du Rhin; celui-là du Cydnus;
> Derrière eux cheminait la Mort, squelette chauve. . . .
>
> (P. 212)

In naming typical paladins, Hugo mentions in order historical, legendary, and imaginary knights: Bernard, Lahire, and Eviradnus, making no distinction between the three categories. The final lines, "Et ces grands chevaliers mêlaient à leurs blasons/ Toute l'immensité des sombres horizons," suggest a "voyage éternel," a voyage of the spirit beyond the geographical limits which are specified: *L'Albe, la Bretagne, le Nil, l'Afrique, l'Inde, Tyr, Héliopolis, Solyme, Césarée.*

This is one of the few poems in the *Légende* that give a *general* image of a single aspect of the Middle Ages, and it is distinct from poems like "Les Quatre Jours d'Elciis" which contain rhetorical indictments. The symbolic heroic figure introduces the medieval cycles that define history in terms of the conflicts of extraordinary men, both good and bad. Paradoxically, these unusual characters symbolize Humanity and the progressive and regressive forces within civilization. "Le siècle de l'individu est le siècle des masses."[23] As in *Notre-Dame de Paris,* the masses are not capable of the individuality or total free will they will reveal later in their revolutionary actions. Nevertheless, in "Les Quatre Jours d'Elciis," the old man warns the kings and clergy that an uprising will come.

> Non, je vous le redis, sire, le grand dormant
> S'éveillera; non, non, Dieu n'est pas mort. O princes,
> Ce peuple, ramassant ses tronçons, ses provinces,
> Tous ses morceaux coupés par vous, pâle, effrayant,
> Se dressera, le front dans la nuée, ayant
> Des jaillissements d'aube aux cils de ses paupières. . . .
>
> (P. 381)

In his exhaustive study of the sources of the medieval poems in the *Légende*, Paul Berret concludes that this is not an "objective" epic, for, in large part, it is a continuation of the social satire of *Les Châtiments*.[24] Placed in the context of nineteenth-century politics, the Middle Ages become, more than ever, an allegory of the contemporary scene with a fixed pattern of reference between the symbolism of particular poems and the general evil which is being attacked. Ratbert is closely linked with Napoléon III, and the murder of Isora should be read in the context of "L'Enfant de la nuit du quatre."[25] Events in "Ratbert," "d'Elciis," and "Félibien" are rooted in the actions of Austria toward Italy.

If the allegory is extended to include the chivalric heroes, we find that they represent Hugo himself. He is the Cid in exile, refusing amnesty, and the isolated Welf or Masferrer, splendid in this defiance. Modifications in the imagery and poetic form of the *Légende* correspond to the increasing personalization within Hugo's concept of chivalry and of the defiant hero. The ideal is represented by "La terre a vu jadis," a symbolic statement of the function of the knight. The specific characters in the *Légende* fall into two general categories, those drawn from historical precedents and those imaginary heroes designated by Hugo himself as medieval. Chronologically, Hugo turned first to the figures of Roland, Charlemagne, Aymeri, and the Cid.

In both "Le Mariage de Roland" and "Aymerillot," heroism is suggested by the action of the poem. Although in the opening stanza of "Le Mariage" the battle between Roland and Olivier is described by imagery which occurs also in "La terre a vu jadis," elsewhere in the poem the two are simply "les héros." "C'est le duel effrayant de deux spectres d'airain,/ Deux fantômes auxquels le démon prête une âme,/ Deux masques dont les trous laissent voir de la flamme" (p. 139). Hugo creates the illusion of furious action through onomatopoeia: "O chocs affreux! terreur! tumulte étincelant!" The opening of the poem leads the reader to believe that the narrative will depict the physical bravery of two ferocious young warriors, but the actual focus is on the pauses in the action. In emphasizing that heroism depends on the naïve determination of each man to "play fair" and that physical bravery is relative between equally matched opponents, Hugo ironically undercuts the popular concept of heroic action in the *chanson de geste*. For example, when Olivier's sword is broken, Roland does not take advantage. "Çà, dit Roland, je suis neveu du roi de France,/ Je dois me comporter en franc neveu de roi./ Quand j'ai mon ennemi désarmé devant moi,/ Je m'arrête" (p. 140). The irony of the final lines brings this battle (which would otherwise carry on interminably) to a perfect conclusion. Olivier suggests that he and Roland should become brothers and that Roland marry his sister. "C'est ainsi que Roland épousa la belle Aude" (p. 143).

The effect of Hugo's poem is entirely different from that of its source, the thirteenth-century epic *Girart de Vienne*. The narrative framework is undoubtedly the form of the medieval poem, even though Hugo got his material second-hand from Jubinal.[26] In the medieval narrative the combat of Olivier and Roland climaxes the long feud between Charlemagne and Girart over the Duchess of Bourgogne, and an angel from God brings the fight to a close by demanding that the two make peace and fight the pagans instead of each other. As part of the agreement, Aude is given to Roland. Hugo uses just this single incident, removes the psychological study and divine intervention, and adds the brief dénouement. Berret claims that this elimination of the supernatural highlights the heroism of the two combatants in the Hugo poem.[27] However, there is a complete contrast between Olivier and Roland in action and in conversation; Hugo's irony underlines this contrast and the adolescent nature of their heroism.

"Aymerillot" provides another interpretation of the hero's role by means of an adaptation of a *chanson de geste*. Relying on Jubinal's version of *Aymeri de Narbonne*,[28] Hugo relates only the first incident of the epic. Charlemagne, returning from Roncevaux, finds all his barons except the youthful Aymeri unwilling to take Narbonne; Aymeri conquers the town and receives it as a fief from the emperor. Once again, the poem extends the interpretation of heroism given in the medieval epic. The central portion of "Aymerillot" does not treat the capture of Narbonne or Aymeri's heroism, but rather the excuses of the barons whom Charlemagne asks to take the town. By means of dialogue and discourse, Hugo suggests that daring heroism is synonymous with youth; however, he makes his point by emphasizing the attitudes of those who are older. "Nous voulons nos foyers, nos logis, nos amours./ C'est ne jouir jamais que conquérir toujours" (p. 145).

In the course of the poem, Charlemagne gains in stature as he asserts his leadership. When he is first introduced before he sees Narbonne and decides it must be won from the Saracens, he is overcome with grief at the death of Roland at Roncevaux. The poem becomes more solemn when Charlemagne, like Barbarossa chastising the Burgraves, berates the cowardice of the barons and laments the deaths of Olivier and Roland.

> Pâle, effrayant, pareil à l'aigle des nuées,
> Terrassant du regard son camp épouvanté,
> L'invincible empereur s'écria: "Lâcheté!
> O comtes palatins tombés dans ces vallées,
> O géants qu'on voyait debout dans les mêlées,
> Devant qui Satan même aurait crié merci,

Olivier et Roland, que n'êtes-vous ici!
Si vous étiez vivants, vous prendriez Narbonne. . . ."

(P. 149)

The next episode is not unexpected as Aymeri, who is compared to David of the Old Testament, steps forward — despite the skepticism about his youth — and volunteers to take Narbonne. The dénouement follows abruptly and is in direct contrast to the foregoing dialogue between Charlemagne and his inactive lords. "Le lendemain Aymery prit la ville."

In choosing the Cid as the central character for "Le Romancero du Cid" (1856), Hugo follows the dictates of his Juvenal-Dante role. Both the characterization of the hero and the poetic form reflect Hugo's extra-literary goal of attacking Napoléon III. A verse form of seven-syllable lines and quatrains suggests the oral *romancero,* but irony is created by discrepancies between the title, which indicates a recounting of heroic action, and the content, a catalog of unheroic actions and attitudes leveled by the Cid against the king.

An older, solitary Cid defines his personal heroism in this bitter monologue addressed to the king Don Sanche, a figure representing all the monarchs whom the historical Cid had served.[29] Rhetoric accentuates the parallel between the isolated, virtuous campeador and Hugo in exile as in the direct address and repetitions of the following passage.

Roi, le Cid que l'âge gagne,
S'aime mieux, en vérité,
Montagnard dans sa montagne
Que roi dans ta royauté.

(P. 105)

A shorter poem from the same period makes the same identification between Hugo and the Cid. Published in the "livre satirique" of *Les Quartre Vents de l'esprit,* "Lorsque j'étais un tout jeune homme pâle" compares the young poet to the Cid armed for battle. When the Muse asks about the youth's armor, he replies that his weapons are "la haine du mal" and "l'amour du juste" and that his shield is "mépris et dédain."

The vituperative progression of language within the "Romancero du Cid" depends on the egocentricity of the Cid who continuously contrasts himself and the king.

Roi, c'est moi qui suis ma cage
Et c'est moi qui suis ma clé;

C'est moi qui ferme mon antre;

Mes rocs sont mes seuls trésors;
Et c'est moi qui me dis: rentre!
Et c'est moi qui me dis: sors!

(P. 92)

As the use of the metaphor of the free, savage animal in this citation implies, the Cid sees himself as justly self-righteous because of the moral qualities of the king who is "jaloux, ingrat, défiant, abject, fourbe, voleur, soudard, couard, moqueur, méchant." For the Cid, as well as for Hugo, the basic attribute of the political hero is personal honor — "cet astre de la nuit noire." The final wish of the Cid is that, when he dies, "On allume à cette étoile/ Le cierge de mon cercueil" (p. 109).

The portrayal of the Spanish hero in "Le Cid Exilé" also owes little to the Middle Ages.[30] The poem falls neatly into two parts, each reflecting a different aspect of Hugo's personal experience. Berret believes that Hugo wrote this piece after having refused Napoléon III's offer of amnesty in August of 1859 (despite the manuscript date of 11 February 1859). In any case, the dominant theme, enunciated in the first part of the poem, is that history justifies the exiled hero, although he may be consigned to oblivion by political decree: "L'exil, est-ce l'oubli vraiment? Une mémoire/ Qu'un prince étouffe est-elle éteinte pour la gloire?" (p. 165). Hugo answers this question with a myth, indicating his faith that history ultimately grants recognition to the exile. A traveler, in search of the "Pic du Midi," travels for three days ("Le genre humain dirait trois siècles") and suddenly catches sight of the terrifying mountain.

Un pignon de l'abîme, un bloc prodigieux
Se dresse, aux lieux profonds mêlant les lieux sublimes;
Sombre apparition de gouffres et de cimes,
Il est là; le regard croit, sous son porche obscur,
Voir le noeud monstrueux de l'ombre et de l'azur,
Et son faîte est un toit sans brouillard et sans voile
Où ne peut se poser d'autre oiseau que l'étoile;
C'est le Pic du Midi.
L'Histoire voit le Cid.
(PP. 165–66)

One might interpret the final hemistich as "L'Histoire voit Hugo."

The second part of the poem presents in a narrative form the king's decision to recall the Cid, the embassy of Don Santos, and the exile's rejection of the invitation to return. Once more, irony is basic to the dénouement of the anecdote. Alphonse's decision to recall the Cid is treated as a mere whim. " 'Ruy Diaz de Bivar revient. Je le rappelle./ Je le veux' " (p. 166). The ambassador explains the king's anger that the

Cid has not shown proper respect to his lord; no vassal has ever greeted his lord "avec un respect plus semblable au mépris" (p. 171). After Don Santos requests that the Cid show more respect to the king, Ruy Diaz de Bivar speaks for the first time, concluding the poem. "— Sire, il faudrait d'abord que vous fissiez en sorte/ Que j'eusse de l'estime en vous parlant à vous" (p. 172).[31]

In the second half of "Le Cid Exilé," description is as important as narrative, for Hugo depicts the plains of Spain and the independent men who inhabit them. He draws upon impressions from his 1843 trip to the Pyrenees[32] and creates a counterpart for the myth of the traveler which he uses earlier in the poem.

> Peu d'herbe; les brebis paissent exténuées;
> Le pâtre a tout l'hiver sur son toit de roseaux
> Le bouleversement farouche des nuées
> Quand les hydres de pluie ouvrent leurs noirs naseaux.
> Ces hommes sont vaillants.
>
> (P. 168)

The Cid finds complete acceptance among such people who live freely and without sham; he in turn is their protector. Like Hugo, he is the champion of social justice, seeing between himself and the inhabitants of the territory of his exile the bond of independent spirits.

> Les rayons du grand Cid sur leurs toits se répandent;
> Il est l'auguste ami du chaume et du grabat;
> Car avec les héros les laboureurs s'entendent;
> L'épée a sa moisson, le soc a son combat.
>
> (P. 168)

Both of these poems on the Cid were not published until the second series of the *Légende,* and, in the final organization of the epic, they are more closely associated with the attack on the monarchy as an institution than with the glorification of the chivalric ideal. On the other hand, "Le Petit Roi de Galice" and "Eviradnus," written in December 1858 and January 1859, are placed immediately following "La terre a vu jadis," and the poems are directly related to one another. Thematically, they treat the hero's rescue of a helpless heir from the hands of usurpers (the "infants d'Asturie" and "Joss" and "Zéno"). Hugo reserves harsh condemnation for the villains of these pieces, describing the would-be destroyers of Mahaud in "Eviradnus" as sterile and rotten. But the heroes dominate these narratives and exemplify that rough, ferocious gleam of light shed by the chivalric ideal. Roland, the last "historical" figure in the medieval poems of the *Légende,* embodies righteous indignation as he attacks the kidnappers of the "petit roi." "J'ai la Colère pour nom," he cries. Eviradnus achieves mythic grandeur beyond even that of the initial phrase — "le Samson chrétien" — which Hugo uses to introduce him.

Hugo's travels in Spain and Germany were a major inspiration for both poems.[33] As a result, décor becomes more than a picturesque setting; the essence of each heroic action is reinforced and amplified by the external atmosphere. The narrative form of "Le Petit Roi" is one of the few heroic *récits* in which Hugo handles the narrative with considerable economy. Unconsciously, he may have been following the model of the *chanson de geste,* for Roland's abrupt appearance and his defeat of the Infants suggests a heroism of action. The story of usurpation is a synthesis of Spanish politics at the end of the eighth and beginning of the ninth centuries;[34] the rescue of the adolescent king is also symbolic of individualistic attempts to combat the decline of order in medieval society.

The outstanding feature of "Le Petit Roi" is the complete accord between the harsh setting, the portrayal of the angry hero, and the ferocious combat. The rough verbal texture underlines this heroism of action and the nature of the countryside.

> On entend dans les pins que l'âge use et mutile
> Lutter le rocher hydre et le torrent reptile;
> Près du petit pré vert pour la halte choisi,
> Un précipice obscur, sans pitié, sans merci,
> Aveugle, ouvre son flanc, plein d'une pâle brume
> Où l'Ybaïchalval, épouvantable, écume.
> De vrais brigands n'auraient pas mieux trouvé l'endroit.
>
> (P. 215)

Roland speaks in a surprisingly sharp, down-to-earth fashion, emphasizing the hardships of the life of active heroism. "Ah! pardieu, s'il est beau d'être prince, c'est rude" (p. 221). And the combat is harsh — "un choc hideux de javelines" — as the single hero is pitted against the ursurpers. "Tous d'un côté; de l'autre, un seul; tragique duel!/ Lutte énorme! combat de l'Hydre et de Michel!" (p. 228).

"Eviradnus" ushers in an entirely different world. The poem contains most of the elements of a gothic romance, set in a Black Forest. Hugo creates a mood of mounting terror in the penetration of the sinister woods, the manor of Corbus, and the banquet hall where Mahaud is to spend the night before she becomes the marquise. "Rien ne parle en ce lieu d'où tout homme s'enfuit./ La terreur, dans les coins accroupie, attend l'hôte" (p. 243). The narrative presents that combination of legend and history expected from a *Castle of Otranto.* According to a legend cited in the poem, each new lord of the manor of Corbus dines alone one evening in the formidable castle; the custom has been in effect for centuries; thus an additional layer of time is added to the already distant medieval past of the *récit*. There is an element of the sensational in Eviradnus's rescue of the capricious Mahaut from her rivals, the German emperor and the Polish king, who plot an ambush in the castle and suffer the catastrophe of death in the gaping abyss beneath the banquet hall. The fact that Eviradnus appears as a specter from among the rows of crested armor in the hall gives the tale an appropriate "supernatural" turn while the attention Hugo gives to describing details of the décor and costumes in the banquet hall also adds to the parallels between the poem and the gothic romance of the *roman terrifiant*.

Eviradnus assumes heroic proportions beyond even Roland. He is a figure of *démesure* before he even acts.

> Quand il songe et s'accoude, on dirait Charlemagne;
> Rôdant, tout hérissé, du bois à la montagne,
> Velu, fauve, il a l'air d'un loup qui serait bon;
> Il a sept pieds de haut comme Jean de Bourbon.
>
> (P. 233)

When Eviradnus eventually raises the visor of his helmet and surprises the plotters, Hugo uses a Homeric simile to describe him. It is almost the last verbal device left to indicate the heroic proportions of this figure.

> Comme sort de la brume
> Un sévère sapin, vieilli dans l'Appenzell,
> A l'heure où le matin au souffle universel
> Passe, des bois profonds balayant la lisière,
> Le preux ouvre son casque, et hors de la visière
> Sa longue barbe blanche et tranquille apparaît.
>
> (P. 263)

In contrast to the economy of the narration of "Le Petit Roi," each element of the adventure in "Eviradnus" is introduced by clusters of images. This expansive technique creates a reverberating effect, a sonority and dense verbal texture, perfectly suited to the nature of this grotesque adventure.[35] Hugo reproduces, for instance, the gutteral sounds of German in drawing upon his memories of his Rhine trip for the description of the castle in its forest setting.[36] His treatment of the empty suits of armor in the banquet hall represents the most protracted elaboration in the poem. The armor, a symbolic and sinister echo of the past, is described by slow-moving lines of echoing vowels and sibilants.

> Ces sphinx ont l'air, au seuil du gouffre où rien ne luit,
> De regarder l'énigme en face dans la nuit,
> Comme si, prêts à faire, entre les bleus pilastres,

Sous leurs sabots d'acier étinceler les astres,
Voulant pour cirque l'ombre, ils provoquaient d'en bas,
Pour on ne sait quels fiers et funèbres combats,
Dans le champ sombre où n'ose aborder la pensée,
La sinistre visière au fond des cieux baissée.

(P. 247)

The insertion into the narrative of the light *chanson*, "Si tu veux, faisons un rêve," underlines the resonance of the rest of the poem.

Other heroic figures in the medieval poems of the *Légende* are not active characters in a symbolic adventure. Their heroism, unlike that of Eviradnus, is not related to the chivalric ideal of the *paladin*. Growing out of Hugo's realization that his political exile and isolation were becoming more or less permanent, each figure is a defiant opponent of tyranny. This fixed symbolic role indicates the sharp tone of the second series of the *Légende* in which most of these figures appear. Their defiance may be verbal and often takes the form of raging discourse. Without fail, the courageous prophet of truth is an old man, representative of the heroes of another age. Elciis, in "Les Quatre Jours d'Elciis" (1857), enunciates the theme of the decline of greatness. "Quelle nuit! N'est-ce pas le plus dur des affronts/ Que nous les preux ayons pour fils eux, les poltrons!" (p. 371). Similarly, Onfroy is called "ce héros d'un autre âge" after he has defied Ratbert, and the theme reoccurs much later in "La Paternité" (1875). "On n'est plus à présent les hommes d'autrefois" (p. 405). A striking example of this verbal defiance is found in "Le Comte Félibien" (1876); as the old man appears, he is acclaimed first as Dante.

L'un crie: Alighieri! c'est lui! c'est l'homme-fée
Qui revient des enfers comme en revint Orphée;
Orphée a vu Pluton, et Dante a vu Satan,
Il arrive de chez les morts; Dante, va-t'en!

(P. 119)

Félibien condemns the murderous atrocities of the sixteenth century and accuses the killers of suppressing the "promesse obscure du destin!" (p. 120).

Masferrer and Welf are heroes of a slightly different coloring; although one is Spanish and the other Scandinavian, both are derived from Job of *Les Burgraves*. Symbolic, too, of defiance, they denounce the present generation by their isolation in an impregnable fortress. Masferrer (1859) is described as a man of solitude, a bandit, who has a strange communication with the savage world of nature. "Calme et formidable," he has "Avec la ronce et l'ombre et l'éclair flamboyant/ Et la trombe et l'hiver de farouches concordes" (p. 392). He rejects with a wave of his hand the offer of the kingship by the cruel lords of northern Spain, "ces noirs seigneurs," who cause misery among the people.

Similarly, Welf (1869) is portrayed as the "protecteur d'un pays inconnu."[37] He rejects all authority, clerical and civil, for he is "un spectre en liberté songeant au fond des nuits" (p. 347). "Rois, l'honneur exista jadis. J'en suis le reste./ C'est bien. Partez. S'il est un bruit que je déteste,/ C'est le bourdonnement inutile des voix" (p. 348). /In the climax to this poetic drama, Welf is captured as he offers aid to a beggar who seeks shelter. His demise is a fitting commentary on the fate of this second group of prophetic heroes in the *Légende*. Representatives of the Titans of the past, they have little authority among a generation of lesser men, but they symbolize the type of man who will reappear in the future.

Although on the highest level the conflict in the Middle Ages was symbolic of man's struggles for moral and spiritual progress, Hugo's personal involvement usually caused him to define the struggle in political terms. Further, his sense of having an all-embracing poetic vision resulted in the epic *démesure* evident in both the conception of characters and the form of his poems. When Hugo is at his best, his grand vision and verbal sonority achieve the proportions of myth; irony and bitter satire are used to good effect. His weakest poetry seems contrived. In "La Confiance du marquis Fabrice," for instance, there is a narrative comparable to that of "Eviradnus." The principal characters are the same: Ratbert, the evil usurper, Fabrice, the aged hero, and Isora, the heiress, but the roles have a different import. Fabrice is described as a star, now extinct "dans un morne brouillard," and he becomes the victim of the unscrupulous machinations of Ratbert who murders Isora. Poetic justice is arbitrarily administered when, as Ratbert watches the decapitation of Fabrice, his own head rolls to the ground.

In order to make clear the ruthlessness of the tyrant, Hugo emphasizes the sentiment and melodrama of the relationship between the grandfather and granddaughter, which is like that of Jean Valjean and Cosette. "Ce vieillard, c'est un chêne adorant une fleur." In "Eviradnus," on the other hand, he creates an atmosphere of visual and verbal terror and grandeur which reinforces the positive heroic act. But "La Confiance du marquis Fabrice" juxtaposes the malicious joy of the king and his underlings with the sentiment surrounding Fabrice and Isora, and the reader becomes painfully aware that the grotesque has been carried too far.

> Il semble qu'on pourrait à peine distinguer
> De ces hommes les loups, les chiennes de ces femmes;
> A travers l'ombre on voit toutes les soifs infâmes,

Le désir, l'instinct vil, l'ivresse aux cris hagards,
Flamboyer dans l'étoile horrible des regards.

(P. 324)

"L'Aigle du casque" (1876), almost the last medieval poem Hugo wrote for the *Légende,* is an interesting exception to the series of heroic conflicts he envisioned. Tiphaine is a part of the chivalric world but he deviates from the ideal because he is without mercy. Hugo does not indict the ferocious warrior on political grounds but portrays the moral "flaw" of Tiphaine who persists in the pursuit of a youth who is by no means his equal.[38] Following a pledge made to his dying grandfather, Jacques at the age of sixteen challenges Tiphaine to fight. When the meeting occurs, Jacques runs away, and the older man refuses three pleas for mercy as he pursues and kills his opponent.

One source for the tale was Jubinal's adaptation of Raoul's chase after Ernaut from *Raoul de Cambrai,* published thirty years earlier, but the more influential source was probably the translation of Bürger's ballad "Le Féroce Chasseur."[39] In this poem the huntsman refuses three times to show mercy; he engages in a relentless pursuit of his victim until he suddenly finds he is being chased by Satanic forces, and the narrative comes to a supernatural conclusion. The influence of the rhythmic ballad form on "L'Aigle du casque" places it apart from most of the other medieval poems of the *Légende.*

The opening lines of "L'Aigle du casque" set the stage for the tragic adventure to follow. "O sinistres forêts, vous avez vu ces ombres/ Passer, l'une après l'autre (p. 291). The setting in Scotland is vague, perhaps because Hugo had not been there, but he returns to the general descriptive *topoi* used in the *Odes et Ballades.* He depicts the old chiefs of Scotland as having the same characteristics as the countryside and then adds a few authoritative names from Moréri's historical dictionary. He emphasizes again the historical distance between the era of the adventure and the time of its poetic recreation. "Ainsi les anciens chefs d'Ecosse et de Northumbre/ Ne sont guère pour nous que du vent et de l'ombre" (p. 292). Then, after setting the stage for the action, Hugo begins it with a single hemistich: "Fanfares. C'est Angus."

Since the conflict is tinged with tragedy, Hugo cites Greek and Ossianic mythology to make the most of the unequal match: the pairs Hercules and Hylas, Polyphemus and Acis are unequal as opposed to Ajax and his equal Mars or Fergus and Fingal. Angus (Jacques) comes nonchalantly to the battle, totally unprepared for the violence which awaits him. Both the rhythm and the imagery change when Tiphaine appears on the scene.

On lit sur son écu, pur comme le matin,
La devise des rois d'Angus: *Christ et Lumière*.
La Jeunesse toujours arrive la première;
Il approche joyeux, fragile, triomphant.

(P. 296)

The trumpet sounds and Tiphaine comes into view.

Et brusquement on sent de l'ombre autour de soi;
Bien qu'on soit sous le ciel, on se croit dans un antre.
Un homme vient du fond de la forêt. Il entre.
C'est Tiphaine.
          C'est lui.

(P. 296)

Once the chase is under way, the key moment in the action is introduced by a Homeric simile, as in "Eviradnus." Angus's sense of being pursued is compared to a dream or nightmare experience. Then the rhythm of the poem increases measurably.

O terreur! et l'enfant, blême, égaré, sans voix,
Court et voudrait se fondre avec l'ombre des bois.
L'un fuit, l'autre poursuit. Acharnement lugubre!
Rien, ni le roc debout, ni l'étang insalubre,
Ni le houx épineux, ni le torrent profond,
Rien n'arrête leur course; ils vont, ils vont, ils vont!

(P. 299)

The chase and the dénouement are handled well. Even Hugo could not hope to maintain the momentum of an infernal chase for long, so he concludes the poem with three successive incidents which flash by and are experienced as though from Tiphaine's horse as Tiphaine rejects all pleas for clemency. He is merciless as he kills Angus, but poetic justice administers a severe punishment to him in return; the eagle on his helmet comes to life and attacks Tiphaine.

The appearance of the "Aigle du casque" among the final poems of the *Légende* indicates the continuity of Hugo's medievalism, despite the variety of poetic forms that suggest the diverse sources of these "medieval" pieces. None of the short poems of the *Ballades* can equal the conception of "L'Aigle du casque," but the later poem stems from an interest in narrative poetry dating back to the early years of Hugo's career. The central figure within this particular narrative exists, not simply as a political example, but as a symbol from the medieval past in the poet's evolving vision of a humane world.

"Le Moyen-Age Mort . . . "

Among Hugo's final publications, the Middle Ages per se receive no attention. The few medieval allusions continue as vehicles for his political and social concerns, climaxing the process which had begun even before the era of *Les Châtiments*. An example which illustrates and recapitulates how medieval motif was adapted to each stage of Hugo's thought and poetic technique is his presentation of Montfaucon, the gallows of Paris, built in the thirteenth century and located outside the city. Hugo found a description of Montfaucon in the second volume of Sauval's *Histoire et recherches des antiquités de la ville de Paris* when he was preparing *Notre-Dame de Paris*. He had first evidenced dislike for the gallows and the hangman in *Han d'Islande*, so that both his taste for the grotesque and his social convictions caused him to retain the image of Montfaucon in the storehouse of his memory.

The theme that social injustice was accepted as a fact of life in fifteenth-century Paris is evident enough in *Notre-Dame*. Hugo situates the final scene at Montfaucon — the discovery of Quasimodo's skeleton joined to Esmeralda in death. The description of Montfaucon is a blending of antiquarian details and poetic suggestiveness. Although Hugo does not specifically relate this setting to the rest of the novel, it brings the social themes of the work to a conclusion.

> Montfaucon était, comme dit Sauval, "le plus ancien et le plus superbe gibet du royaume". Entre les faubourgs du Temple et de Saint-Martin, à environ cent soixante toises des murailles de Paris, à quelques portées d'arbalète de la Courtille, on voyait au sommet d'une éminence douce, insensible, assez élevée pour être aperçue de quelques lieues à la ronde, un édifice de forme étrange, qui ressemblait assez à un cromlech celtique, et où il se faisait aussi des sacrifices.[1]

Hugo pictures the stark silhouette of the gallows against the sky — "un horrible profil." "Il suffisait de ce gibet présent là pour faire de tous les environs des lieux sinistres."[2] This recreation in words of a mental image illustrates the way Hugo assimilated a detail from his poetic vision. He also sketched Montfaucon as he described it, a somber megalith isolated against the horizon.[3]

In the course of his political education, Hugo gradually associated the executioner with the king, the emperor, and the Church. For instance, "Ecrit en 1846," a defense of his changing political ideas published in *Les Contemplations,* pictures the evil of revolutions as necessary to accomplish an eternal good. Revolutions purge the horrors of past reigns, including the sufferings of the Middle Ages caused by a ruler like Louis XI and his executioner Tristan.[4]

As a result of his opposition to authoritarian institutions, Hugo entitled one poem of *La Légende des Siècles* "Montfaucon" (1858), publishing it as part of the section "Après les Dieux, les Rois." In the first part of the poem, he rewrites history, attributing the building of the *gibet* to Philippe le Bel in the fourteenth century. Taking the legend that the king offered the papacy to Bertrand de Got (Clément V) during an interview in the woods of Saint-Jean d'Angély, Hugo has the archbishop suggest that the way to maintain power is by means of the gallows. The second part of the poem is a depiction of Montfaucon in all its horror and of its victims, the names of whom Hugo lifted from Moréri's dictionary. In contrast to the description in *Notre-Dame,* Montfaucon is now brought to life as a monster, and Hugo links its monstrous aspects with the architectural image of the subterranean staircase. "Fauve, il traîne/ Sur sa pente, d'où sort une horreur souterraine,/ Son funeste escalier qui dans la mort finit."[5] Written in the spirit of Juvenal-Dante, "Montfaucon" is Hugo's most intense concretization of his vision of the medieval gallows.

By the time of the publication of *Les Quatre Vents de l'esprit* in 1881, Montfaucon is simply a reference. However, Hugo develops a new context for the allusion when he catalogues history's most evil figures in the poem "Ils sont toujours là" (1875). Montfaucon here represents man's inhumanity to his fellow man (Cain killing Abel), and the symbol of the gallows is raised from a political level to a larger moral plane.

> Il [Caïn] rit de voir partout le glaive
> Et, sur toutes les croix qu'élève
> A tous ses étages Babel,
> Aux gibets qu'on hait ou révère,
> A Montfaucon comme au Calvaire,
> L'immense cadavre d'Abel.[6]

During the decade of the 1870s Hugo's attitude toward the Middle Ages became blacker than at any other time during his career; the ambivalence of his youthful enthusiasm now turned into hate. Although he still admired gothic architecture, he treated medieval ruins and the interest of the antiquarian in the past with irony. In *Margarita* (1869), part of the "livre dramatique" of *Les Quatre Vents de l'esprit*, the Duke Gallus expresses cynical *ennui* when he views the fortress of the Baron of Holburg.

> — Des ancêtres cassés. Des preux estropiés.
> Force héros sans nez, perdus dans les décombres.
> Ce mélange imposant de Charlemagnes sombres,
> De Barberousses morts, de Christs, de Jéhovahs,
> De saints, que le vulgaire appelle des gravats.
> L'auguste bric-à-brac, épars sous la fougère,
> Que l'histoire plus tard met sur son étagère.
> Une commission de savants trouverait
> A camper dans cette herbe énormément d'attrait.[7]

Specifically, Hugo's hatred of the Middle Ages must be understood as a hatred of the institutions of the period which obstructed man's progress. And in the 1870s his dislike for nineteenth-century dogmatism and dictatorship caused him to forget that he had been using the Middle Ages as a metaphor for contemporary politics. The historical distance between past and present now disappears in the few allusions Hugo makes to the earlier period. All obstructions to progress are medieval, and they have outlived their time, for the Revolution had destroyed the Middle Ages.

As a result, when the treaty with Prussia was signed in 1871, "Destruction de la Colonne. Acceptation du traité prussien" suggests Hugo's national pride in the past accomplishments of the revolutionary and Napoleonic periods which led to the destruction of monarchies and the liberation of the *peuple*. The column speaks:

> Peuple, quels sont mes torts? les trônes en éclats,
> L'Europe labourée en tous sens par la France,
> La bataille achevée en vaste délivrance,
> Le moyen-âge mort, les préjugés proscrits.[8]

Hugo would not want France to turn back the clock of time, for the medieval past has been destroyed once and for all. He would, however, urge that it guard the memory of the moment the abolition of the Middle Ages took place.

The opinion "J'aime la cathédrale et non le moyen-âge"[9] is to be found in another poem from the early 1870s, "Muse, un nommé Ségur. . . ." The context of the statement is an answer to an episcopal attack on *Les Misérables*. It highlights Hugo's anticlericalism and antidogmatism, which became stronger as the attempt was made by Jules Ferry to secularize French education after 1870.

> Pape, Dieu, ce n'est pas le même personnage.

J'aime la cathédrale et non le moyen-âge.
Qu'est-ce qu'un dogme, un culte, un rite? Un objet d'art.
Je puis l'admirer; mais s'il égare un soudard,
S'il grise un fou, s'il tue un homme, je l'abhorre.[10]

Certainly, it is fair to conclude that Hugo hated the Middle Ages when he thought of the Church or the Monarchy. But this passage illustrates well the blurring that occurred in his vision of the period late in his career. In these bitter allusions, he no longer turns to the Middle Ages to represent the injustices of his own time — as he does in *La Légende des Siècles*. Rather, he looks for vestiges of the past which carry over into the present — vestiges of obscurantism, dogmatism, and authoritarianism — and these he labels medieval.

Quatrevingt-treize, Hugo's last novel, stands out as an important example of the negative medievalism of his final years. Here medieval motif is an organic part of the historic conflict which exists on several levels in the novel. In *Notre-Dame de Paris*, Hugo did not link his plot to the changes he implies were taking place in fifteenth-century Paris. Subsequently, he emphasized the conflicting forces in medieval history by means of symbolic figures. But in *Le Rhin, Les Burgraves,* and *La Légende des Siècles*, Hugo never depicted the figure who feels *within himself* the conflicts of historical movement. This he does in *Quatrevingt-treize,* and the novel marks a further development in Hugo's use of medieval motif within the narrative mode.

A comparison of *Quatrevingt-treize* with Walter Scott's conception of the historical novel suggests that Hugo's work follows the same general outline and does it with surprising economy. Hugo has captured the moment of change as one culture or era dies and another emerges; his fictional characters participate in the historical conflict, and the historical figures remain on the periphery.[11] The revolt of the royalists in the Vendée against the power of the Convention in Paris marks the last effort of dying feudalism to obstruct the irrevocable, harsh, cleansing force of the Revolution. The symbolic figures of Lantenac, the unbending royalist, and Cimourdain, the priest who is the agent of the Revolution under orders to show no pity to the insurgents, represent the irreconcilable clash between past and future. Caught between these extremes is the officer Gauvain, nephew of Lantenac and former pupil of Cimourdain. Gauvain is a man of divided loyalties; he must choose whether to capture and kill Lantenac. If he does kill Lantenac, he denies his past and his family and affirms his allegiance to the Revolution.

In this historical tension, medieval motifs work to highlight the theme that the dark, feudal past must give way to the future. The royalist-Catholic revolt takes place in the forest of the Vendée. "Il y avait alors en Bretagne sept forêts horribles. La Vendée, c'est la révolte-prêtre. Cette révolte a eu pour auxiliaire la forêt. Les ténèbres s'entr'aident."[12] At the same time, Hugo emphasizes that the forests retain the atmosphere of the Celtic, magic past and the legends from this past are as real as history in the minds of the inhabitants. The Breton peasants live a subterranean life in these forests, and the entire Vendean revolt is born of a blindness engendered by the "tragic forests" of the past (pp. 219–29). People had always fled to these regions for refuge. "De là les tanières et reptiles creusées sous les arbres. Cela datait des druides, et quelques-unes de ces cryptes étaient aussi anciennes que les dolmens. Les larves de la légende et les monstres de l'histoire, tout avait passé sur ce noir pays" (p. 223). There is an echo from Marchangy's *La Gaule poétique* in Hugo's portrayal of these dark forests. Marchangy describes at length this region. "Les forêts druidiques n'étaient éclairées que par des rayons vacillants et presque éteints, par des reflets aussi pâles que les lueurs d'une lampe sépulcrale."[13] Against this somber backdrop Hugo places the noise and vitality of the streets of Paris, "l'aspect grandiose et farouche des commencements," which are recreated in the section preceding this introduction to the Vendée (p. 132; see pp. 123–33).

The battle between the revolutionaries of Paris and the Catholic royalists is later described as an interfamily struggle because Hugo personalizes the historical tension in the character of Gauvain. The conflict is called medieval precisely because it exists on a family level (p. 380). Speaking of the Tourgue, the ancestral fortress and home of Gauvain's family which the officer must attack because Lantenac finally takes refuge there, Hugo concludes that "cette vieille demeure revenait, en pleine révolution française, à ses habitudes féodales. Les guerres entre parents sont toute l'histoire du moyen âge; les Etéocles et les Polynices sont gothiques aussi bien que grecs, et Hamlet fait dans Elseneur ce qu'Oreste a fait dans Argos" (p. 317).

The battle for the medieval Tourgue, "une bastille de province," represents both the personal and impersonal aspects of historical conflict. Hugo portrays Gauvain's internal conflict in terms of this fortress. Like the cathedral in *Notre Dame,* the Tourgue is as important as any central character in the novel, but unlike the church, it is a catalyst for the interiorization of Gauvain's misgivings about the ruthless demands of the revolutionary cause. The fortress has two facets, the tower (the savage aspect) and the library (civilization).[14] In his conservative extremism, Lantenac, although a Gauvain, would have paradoxically done away with the Tourgue, sacrificing it for the cause of the Vendée. But young Gauvain recoils from destroying the library, symbolic of the best of the past and his indebtedness to that past.

La Tourgue était le manoir de famille des Gauvain; c'est de cette tour que mouvaient tous leurs fiefs de Bretagne, de même que les fiefs de France mouvaient de la tour du Louvre; les souvenirs domestiques des Gauvain étaient là; lui-même, il y était né; les fatalités tortueuses de la vie l'amenaient à attaquer, homme, cette muraille vénérable qui l'avait protégé enfant. Serait-il impie envers cette demeure jusqu'à la mettre en cendres? (P. 316)

In the end, Imânus, the ruthless exterminator of men for the forces of the Vendée, sets fire to the library, and both sides become responsible for the destruction of the center of the Tourgue.

The dénouement grows directly out of Hugo's use of the Tourgue as a focal point for Gauvain's torment. Moved by Lantenac's willingness to sacrifice himself in order to rescue the children trapped in the burning library, Gauvain allows his uncle to escape while he in turn faces the guillotine for refusing to follow the directives of Paris that no enemy be spared death. In the chapter "Gauvain pensif," Hugo interiorizes the psychological conflict in the hero as he, like Jean Valjean in "tempête sous un crâne," makes a decision involving his own destiny. Gauvain's interior debate about the Tourgue indicates moral sensitivity and prepares the reader for self-sacrifice. Caught between the forces of feudalism and revolution, Gauvain acts in the name of humanity for the sake of a future that will not need the absolutes of revolution. Yet, as the novel ends and Cimourdain orders his execution, Gauvain remains the victim of the tragic confrontation between the Tourgue and the guillotine. The Tourgue no longer symbolizes historic conflict; it represents the "inextricable complication gothique" of a past which has been conquered.

Elle [la Tourgue] avait dominé de sa figure funeste cette forêt, elle avait eu dans cette ombre quinze siècles de tranquillité farouche, elle avait été dans ce pays l'unique puissance, l'unique respect et l'unique effroi; elle avait régné; elle avait été, sans partage, la barbarie; et tout à coup elle voyait se dresser devant elle et contre elle, quelque chose, — plus que quelque chose, — quelqu'un d'aussi horrible qu'elle, la guillotine. (P. 484)

The literary use of the Tourgue in this novel written in 1872 is even more striking when one realizes that Hugo drew upon his mental images of the Tour Mélusine of the château at Fougères he and Juliette Drouet had visited in 1836.[15] This total integration of décor with the historical forces at work in *Quatrevingt-treize* provides a fitting conclusion to a process of evolution that had begun with *Han d'Islande* where the picturesque ruins are simply vestiges of an exotic past which stimulate the hero to sentimental responses. Above all, the Tourgue highlights the ambivalence of Hugo's medievalism, which dates back primarily to *Notre-Dame de Paris*. Despite the hatred for certain aspects of medieval society he expressed in the 1870s, Hugo the creative artist with extraordinary powers of memory and imagination could never totally relinquish his Romantic vision of the Middle Ages.

A medieval aesthetic of the flamboyant gothic, the grotesque, and the sinister ruin became assimilated into Hugo's personal taste. The décor of Hauteville House, a blend of styles ranging from *chinois* to *gothique,* is evidence that Hugo could not have been attracted by the simplicity of much of medieval art.[16] He despaired at both the passing of late gothic architecture in *Notre-Dame* and the disappearance of the baroque in *Quatrevingt-treize* when he wrote that "après les éblouissantes orgies de forme et de coleur du dix-huitième siècle, l'art s'est mis à la diète, et ne se permettait plus que la ligne droite. Ce genre de progrès aboutit à la laideur" (p. 187). Hugo chose from the Middle Ages those aspects which harmonized with his taste just as he rejected aspects of its culture on political and religious grounds.

Hugo's attraction to Dante, the great emperors, the burgraves, and the chevaliers can also be attributed to his personality. The "Ego Hugo" in all its roles — *mage, visionnaire, prophète, homme politique, exilé* — found aspects of itself in these heroic figures which could not be rejected in the poet's later years despite his gradual conviction that the Middle Ages as a whole were scarcely illuminated by any form of human progress. Inheriting, then, the popular conception of the medieval period which existed during the pre-Romantic and Romantic periods and, in turn, helping mold that taste, Hugo rejected the concept of a homogeneous, ideal Christian medieval era. He personalized and transformed certain elements of Romantic medievalism.

Medieval motif serves as a touchstone for an understanding of Hugo's gradual perception of the concept of historical change and the portrayal of this change in literary form. Before *Notre Dame,* the Middle Ages were a distant, exotic past, reflected in the conventional images and formal experiments of the *Ballades.* But with his novel of fifteenth-century Paris, Hugo documented and tried to recapture the color of a waning era. He did not, however, produce a totally integrated novel, for there is a dichotomy between the poetic reality of the medieval atmosphere and the melodramatic plot.

With *Le Rhin* and *Les Burgraves,* history (now a term implying both recorded history and legend) became much more than a distant moment to be recaptured. Hugo envisioned the dynamism within the Middle Ages as the struggle between the forces that would unify or disrupt civilization. He projected this antithetical conflict into the mythic figures of Barbarossa and Job, but given the historical conflict in *Les Burgraves,* there is a dichotomy in the literary form. Conscious that his interpretation of the past could influence his contemporaries, Hugo created a drama that functions on two levels, as a melodrama geared to the popular audience and as a series of poetic arias which would convey his political ideas by means of a rhetoric of images.

By means of the epic scope of *La Légende des Siècles,* Hugo conveyed both the dynamic conflict within the Middle Ages and the movement of history from the past toward an apocalyptic future. The historical distance between the medieval past and the empire of Napoléon III is again apparent when the Middle Ages serve as an allegory of contemporary injustice. But in those cases in which Hugo allows the past to speak for itself through its symbolic figures, as in "L'Aigle du casque," he creates narrative poetry which exists in and for itself as a self-contained rhythmic whole. The distance between the medieval past and the present finally disappears on the fictive level in *Quatrevingt-treize* where Hugo recreates a moment in time when man thinks he is destroying the past and creating a new future. The Tourgue exists finally as a battered symbol of the Middle Ages which are now a memory.

The following abbreviations are used in the notes and bibliography:

MLN	*Modern Language Notes*
MLQ	*Modern Language Quarterly*
n.a.fr.	Nouvelles acquisitions françaises
NRF	*Nouvelle Revue Française*
RHLF	*Revue d'Histoire Littéraire de la France*
RLC	*Revue de Littérature Comparée*
RSH	*Revue des Sciences Humaines*

Notes

Chapter 1

1. Preface to *Dessins de Victor Hugo* engraved by Paul Chenay, rpt. in *Oeuvres complètes,* ed. Jean Massin, 18 vols. (Paris: Club français du livre, 1967–70) 18: 3. This citation includes the subsequent quotation in the paragraph.
2. Michelet uses the phrase in the introduction to volume 7 of his *Histoire de France* (Paris: Hachette, 1833–55).
3. Robert F. Turner, *The Sixteenth Century in Victor Hugo's Inspiration* (New York: Columbia University Press, 1934), p. 2.
4. (1948; rpt. Paris: Albin Michel, 1969), pp. 263–69.
5. Van Tieghem, *Le Romantisme,* p. 449.
6. Ibid. p. 268.
7. Alice Chard, *A Dream of Order: The Medieval Ideal in Nineteenth-Century English Literature* (Lincoln: University of Nebraska Press, 1970), p. 1.
8. "Critique," 1851–1873, of *Tas de pierres* in *Océan. Tas de pierres, Oeuvres complètes,* 45 vols. (Paris: Ollendorff, Albin Michel, 1904–52): 354. References in the notes to individual volumes of the two sets of *Oeuvres complètes* will henceforth be distinguished by year of publication.
9. E.D. Hirsch, Jr., *Wordsworth and Schelling: A Typological Study of Romanticism* (New Haven: Yale University Press, 1960), p. 5.
10. Morse Peckham uses the term in "Toward a Theory of Romanticism," reprinted in part in *Romanticism: Points of View,* eds. Robert F. Gleckner and Gerald E. Enscoe (Englewood Cliffs, N.J.: Prentice-Hall, 1962), pp. 212–27; see particularly p. 219.
11. An example would be Henri Peyre's "The Originality of French Romanticism," *Symposium* 23 (1969): 333–45; and "Romantisme français et romantismes étrangers" in his *Qu'est-ce que le romantisme?* (Paris: Presses universitaires, 1971), pp. 45–66.
12. *PMLA* 39 (1924): 229–53, reprinted in his *Essays in the History of Ideas* (New York: Putnam, Capricorn, 1960), pp. 228–53.
13. An example is found in Henry H.H. Remak's "West European Romanticism: Definition and Scope" in *Comparative Literature: Method and Perspective,* eds. Newton P. Stallknecht and Horst Frenz (Carbondale: Southern Illinois University Press, 1961), pp. 223–59.
14. *The Idea of History,* (New York: Oxford University Press, Galaxy, 1956), p. 87.
15. Morse Peckham uses the terms "positive romanticism" and "negative romanticism" in "Toward a Theory of Romanticism" in *Romanticism: Points of View,* pp. 219–26.

16. Chard, *A Dream of Order,* p. 40. The text from *Ivanhoe* is quoted on pp. 38–39.

17. *La Légende des Siècles, La Fin de Satan, Dieu,* ed. J. Truchet, Pléiade Edition (Paris: Gallimard, 1950), p. 211.

18. When comparing eighteenth- and nineteenth-century medievalism in France, Lionel Gossman has commented that "the popular element in the culture of the Middle Ages, from which the eighteenth-century scholars had held themselves somewhat aloof, was at last recognized and made an object of study." *Medievalism and the Ideologies of the Enlightenment: The World and Work of La Curne de Sainte-Palaye* (Baltimore: The Johns Hopkins Press, 1968), p. 333.

Chapter 2

1. For a general discussion see Edmond Estève, "Le Moyen âge dans la littérature du XVIIIe siècle," *Revue de l'Université de Bruxelles* 29 (1923–34): 353–82; René Lanson, *Le Goût du moyen âge en France au XVIIIe siècle* (Paris and Brussels: Van Oest, 1926); and Marcel Aubert, "Le Romantisme et le Moyen Age," in *Le Romantisme et l'art* (Paris: Laurens, 1928), pp. 23–48.

2. Gossman, *Medievalism,* passim.

3. Gossman, *Medievalism,* p. 273. Richard Hurd, for example, used Sainte-Palaye for his *Letters on Chivalry and Romance.* See Friedrich Meinecke, *Historism: The Rise of a New Historical Outlook,* trans., J.E. Anderson (New York: Herder and Herder, 1972), pp. 209–12.

4. Gossman, *Medievalism,* pp. 283–86, 290–95.

5. Quoted by Gossman in *Medievalism,* p. 255.

6. See, for instance, Edmond Huguet, "Quelques Sources de 'Notre-Dame de Paris,' " *RHLF* 8 (1901): 48–79, 425–55, 622–49.

7. Maurice Souriau comments on Hugo's citation of *Le Roman de la Rose* in his edition of *La Préface de Cromwell* (Paris: Boivin, 1897), p. 209.

8. *L'Enfer, poème du Dante,* 2 vol. (London and Paris: P.-F. Didot le jeune, 1785).

9. "Quelques Romans chez nos aïeux," *Journal du Dimanche,* 1 November 1846, p. 6. A general discussion is given by Dorothy A. Doolittle, "The Relations Between Literature and Medieval Studies in France from 1820–1860" (O.P., Originally a Ph.D. diss., Bryn Mawr, 1933).

10. Estève, "Le Moyen âge," p. 380.

11. Detailed studies of the genre troubadour have been published by Fernand Baldensperger, "Le Genre troubadour" in vol. 1 of *Etudes d'histoire littéraire* (Paris: Hachette, 1907): 110–46; and by Henri Jacoubet, *Le Comte de Tressan et les origines du genre troubadour* (Paris: Presses universitaires, 1923); and *Le Genre troubadour et les origines françaises du romantisme* (Paris: Les Belles-Lettres, 1929).

12. *Génie du christianisme,* chronology and introduction by Pierre Reboul, 2 vols. (Paris: Garnier-Flammarion, 1966), 1:44.

13. On Ossianism see Paul Van Tieghem, *Le Préromantisme,* 2nd ed., 3 vols. (Paris: SFELT, 1948), 1: 197–287 and *Ossian en France,* 2 vols. (Paris: F. Rieder, 1917).

14. *Génie du christianisme*, 2: 44–45.

15. Chateaubriand's justification of the epic over drama and his admiration of Dante are also of relevance to Hugo's medievalism.

16. Adèle Hugo, *Victor Hugo raconté par un témoin de sa vie*, 2 vols. (Paris: A. Lacroix, 1863), 2: 5.

17. Géraud Venzac, *Les Origines religieuses de Victor Hugo* (Paris: Blaud et Gay, 1955), p. 370.

18. "La Vendée" (1819), "Le Repos libre" (1823), "Le Dernier Chant" (1823), "A M. de Chateaubriand" (1824), and "Le Génie" (1820) all contain specific references to Chateaubriand or epigraphs from *Les Martyrs*.

19. Brunetière's comment that Chateaubriand alone gave to Hugo "le goût du moyen âge, de ses moeurs et de son art" and also inspired the form of the *Ballades* does not seem accurate. *Victor Hugo*, 2nd ed., 2 vols. (Paris: Hachette, 1906), 1: 61–62.

20. *Correspondance: 1815–1882*, 2 vols. (Paris: Calmann-Levy, 1896–1898), 1: 19, hereafter cited as *Correspondance*.

21. On Hugo and Germany see Charles Dédéyan, *Victor Hugo et l'Allemagne*, 2 vols. (Paris: Minard, 1964–65).

22. *De l'Allemagne*, 2nd ed., 3 vols. (Paris: H. Nicolle, 1814), 1:3.

23. Hugo cites *De l'Allemagne* in an epigraph to chapter eleven of the novel.

24. *De l'Allemagne*, 2: 253–55.

25. *La Gaule poétique*, 3rd ed., 8 vols. (Paris: C.-F. Patris, 1819), 1: 1–2.

26. Pierre Albouy discusses interest in the supernatural and in myth in *La Création mythologique chez Victor Hugo* (Paris: J. Corti, 1964), pp. 23–59; Marchangy is treated on p. 30.

27. *La Gaule poétique*, 3: 4.

28. "Notice," dated 1837, to the *Oeuvres* of Charles-Hubert Millevoye (Paris: Garnier, 1865), p. 15.

29. C.W. Thompson, *Victor Hugo and the Graphic Arts (1820–1833)* (Geneva and Paris: Droz, 1970), pp. 36–37 and Jean-Bertrand Barrère, *La Fantaisie de Victor Hugo*, 3 vols. (Paris: J. Corti, 1949-1960), 1: 106. Hugo owned at least three volumes of the *Voyages pittoresques;* they are listed in an account for 1833 (Bibliothèque Nationale, n.a.fr., 13443) and in the catalogue for the sale of Hugo's belongings in 1852. *Catalogue sommaire d'un bon MOBILIER* (Paris: Maulde et Renou, 1852), p. 8.

30. *Romances historiques*, trans. and ed. Abel Hugo (Paris: Pélicier, 1822), pp. xi–lv.

31. Van Tieghem, *Le Préromantisme*, 1: 7–8, 75–191.

32. Simone Pées, "L'Origine de la couleur locale scandinave dans le 'Han d'Islande' de Victor Hugo," *RLC* 9 (1929): 261–84.

33. *Oeuvres poétiques*, ed. Pierre Albouy, Pléiade Edition, 2 vols. (Paris: Gallimard, 1964–67), 1: 87, hereafter cited as *Oeuvres poétiques*.

34. *La Fantaisie*, 1: 52. Pierre-Georges Castex gives the background of gothic fiction in France in *Le Conte fantastique en France de Nodier à Maupassant* (Paris: J. Corti, 1951).

35. Quoted in *Victor Hugo raconté*, 2: 41–42. For Hugo's use of Scott, consult Sister M. Irene O'Connor, *A Study of the Sources of Han d'Islande and Their Significance in the Development of Victor Hugo* (Washington, D.C.: Catholic University of America Press, 1942), pp. 43–63.

36. Barrère, *La Fantaisie*, 1: 53.

37. Richard B. Grant labels *Han d'Islande* a romance in *Perilous Quest: Image, Myth and Prophecy in the Narratives of Victor Hugo* (Durham, N.C.: Duke University Press, 1968).

38. *Han d'Islande* in *Oeuvres complètes, Roman,* I (1910): 164–65; all pagination given subsequently in the text will refer to this edition.

39. *Hugo, l'homme et l'oeuvre,* new ed. (Paris: Hatier, 1959), p. 23.

40. André Maurois, *Olympio ou la vie de Victor Hugo* (Paris: Hachette, 1954), p. 110; *La Fantaisie*, 1: 54–56; and Raouf Simaïka, *L'Inspiration épique dans les romans de Victor Hugo* (Geneva and Paris: Droz and Minard, 1962), pp. 25–27. In the first poem of the *Feuilles d'Automne,* dated 1830, Hugo speaks of hiding his love and sorrow "Dans le coin d'un roman ironique et railleur" which Pierre Albouy interprets as *Han (Oeuvres poétiques*, 1: 718 and 1340–41).

41. The source of Hugo's ideas on hanging is discussed by M. Larroutis in "J. de Maistre et V. Hugo: le bourreau dans *Han d'Islande," RHLF* 62 (1962): 573–75.

42. For references to the *Edda*s, see pp. 39 and 66; for mythological and historical names, pp. 46, 60, 62, 66–67, and 149.

43. I discuss Hugo and Eckstein in my article, "Victor Hugo, the Baron von Eckstein, and the 'Profondeur des Allemands,' " *RLC* 43 (1969): 459–78.

44. *Annales de la littérature et des arts,* 9 (1822): 172–79 and 232–47.

45. Quoted in "Revue de la critique," in *Han d'Islande*, p. 352.

46. Doolittle, "Literature and Medieval Studies," pp. 7–22; and Eunice M. Schenck, *La Part de Charles Nodier dans la formation des idées romantiques de Victor Hugo jusqu'à la Préface de Cromwell* (Paris: Champion, 1914), passim.

47. Thompson, *Victor Hugo and the Graphic Arts,* p. 37.

Chapter 3

1. *Le Drapeau Blanc* (2 January 1824), p. 2.

2. "De la littérature dramatique chez les modernes," *Le Catholique* 2 (1826): 40–41.

3. Ibid.

4. *Oeuvres poétiques,* 1: 1213.

5. *Victor Hugo* (Paris: Hachette, 1893), pp. 46–50.

6. *La Fantaisie,* 1: 101–10.

7. For a discussion of architecture, the 1825 voyages, and the *Odes et Ballades,* see Jean Mallion, *Victor Hugo et l'art architectural* (Grenoble: Allier, 1962), pp. 39–49.

8. *La Fantaisie,* 1: 107.

9. *Oeuvres poétiques,* 1: 1213.

10. *Oeuvres poétiques,* 1: 475-76.

11. *Correspondance,* 1: 246.

12. I discuss the evolution of Hugo's interpretation of gothic architecture in my article, "The Political Evolution of Victor Hugo's Gothic Vision," *MLQ* 34 (1973): 272–82. Jean Gaudon gives an excellent analysis of the relation

between art and nature in Hugo's aesthetic in *Le Temps de la Contemplation* (Paris: Flammarion, 1969), pp. 89–102.

13. *Correspondance*, 1: 249.

14 The phrase is used in a letter to Victor Pavie in 1827. *Correspondance*, 1: 68.

15. *Oeuvres complètes, En Voyage*, II (1910): 12.

16. Many of these articles have been reprinted by Pierre Trahard in *Le Romantisme défini par le Globe* (Paris: Les Presses françaises, 1924).

17. *Oeuvres poétiques*, 1: 270.

18. On Schlegel in France, see Chetana Nagavajara, *August Wilhelm Schlegel in Frankreich: Sein Anteil an der Französischen Literaturkritik 1807–1835* (Tübingen: Niemeyer, 1966); on Hugo, pp. 138–43; see also my "Victor Hugo, the Baron von Eckstein and the 'Profondeur des Allemands,' " passim. Edmond Eggli discusses Nodier and Schlegel in *Le Débat romantique en France: 1813–1816* (Paris: Les Belles Lettres, 1933), pp. 112–15.

Schlegel's ideas about gothic architecture, though more influential than those of his brother Friedrich, were less original. Friedrich was closely connected with the Boisserée brothers for a time and echoes both them and Goethe. See Nikolaus Pevsner, *Some Architectural Writers of the Nineteenth Century* (Oxford: Clarendon Press, 1972), pp. 12–14. Eckstein published a review of Sulpice Boisserée's study of the cathedral at Cologne in *Le Drapeau Blanc* (6 January 1824). Gottfried Salomon, *Das Mittelalter als Ideal in der Romantik* (Munich: Drei Masken, 1922), pp. 32–36, discusses the gothic revival in Germany.

19. *Oeuvres poétiques*, 1: 281.

20. Ibid.

21. Doolittle, "Literature and Medieval Studies" p. 25. Henri François Bauer, in *Les Ballades de Victor Hugo: Leurs origines françaises et étrangères* (Paris: Champion, 1936), indicates that the *ballades* derive in almost every case from the genre troubadour (pp. 120–22).

22. Jacoubet, *Le Genre troubadour*, pp. 133–34.

23. *Oeuvres poétiques*, 1: 179. All subsequent quotations from the *Odes et Ballades* and page references will be from this edition.

24. He uses the notion in "Le Beau serviteur du Vrai" in *William Shakespeare*, for instance.

25. G. Defaux ("Renaissance poétique nationale et influences allemandes dans les *Odes et Ballades*," *Revue de l'Université d'Ottawa*, 41 [1971]: 5–24) says that Hugo *nationalized* the ballad by making the medieval element dominant.

26. Paul Zumthor, "Le Moyen Age de Victor Hugo" in *Oeuvres complètes* (1967) 4: xiii.

27. "Le Géant" and "A Trilby . . . " date from March and April, 1825, but these poems repeat themes already present in the poems of 1823–24.

28. *Le Rhin, Oeuvres complètes, En Voyage*, I (1906): 179, hereafter cited as *Le Rhin*.

29. In "A un passant," Hugo recites the possible events which could occur during the fearful hours of the night, and these include the *sabbat*. In this poem, the "magique château" serves as a setting for the infernal.

30. An earlier ode, "Le Chant du tournoi" (1824), also reflects the taste for epic action and the chivalric ideal.

31. Barrère quotes Nodier in the *Journal des Débats* (7 March 1818) in *La Fantaisie,* 1: 133.

32. Thompson, *Victor Hugo and the Graphic Arts,* shows the evolution of the spiral image in Hugo's writing until 1833 (pp. 98–112).

33. On Hugo's use of illustrations from painting, see Thompson, *Victor Hugo and the Graphic Arts,* pp. 54–59.

34. Bibliothèque Nationale, n.a.fr. 13393, fol. 117. This passage seems to come from the period 1826–28.

35. *La Préface de Cromwell,* p. 191. Pagination in the text is from Souriau's edition.

36. Wolfgang Kayser summarizes Hugo's view of the grotesque, relating it to German thought, in *The Grotesque in Art and Literature,* trans., Ulrich Weisstein (1963; rpt. New York: McGraw-Hill, 1966), pp. 56–59. Note Hugo's example of Dante's use of the grotesque in the paragraph which follows.

37. A. Counson, *Dante en France* (Erlangen and Paris: F. Junge and Fonte-moing, 1906), p. 93.

38. Thompson, *Victor Hugo and the Graphic Arts,* p. 105; and Luigi Benedetto, "Victor Hugo e Dante," *Lettere Italiane,* 20 (1968): 41.

39. *Corinne ou l'Italie* (Paris: Didot, n.d.), p. 30.

40. "A André Chénier," ll. 21–24, *Les Contemplations,* ed. Joseph Vianey, new edition, 3 vols. (Paris: Hachette, 1922), 3: 35.

41. "Le Ravin," "Malédiction," "Les Djinns," and "Rêverie."

42. *Toute la lyre,* 1, *Oeuvres complètes, Poésie,* XII (1935): 146. See also Thompson, *Victor Hugo and the Graphic Arts,* p. 67.

43. *Oeuvres poétiques,* 1: 580–81. Subsequent pagination for the preface and poems of *Les Orientales* will refer to this edition.

44. *Oeuvres poétiques,* 1: 1318.

45. Amedée Pichot wrote Hugo in 1828 that "le bruit a couru que vous écrivez un roman: Si cela est, si vous n'êtes point fixé sur votre éditeur, je vous indique Charles Gosselin." Bibliothèque Nationale, n.a.fr., 13404, fol. 5.

Chapter 4

1. The sources of Hugo's ideas for the ages of humanity and of poetry have been much discussed. It seems likely that he knew Quinet's translation of Herder, *Idées sur la philosophie de l'histoire de l'humanité,* 3 vol. (Paris: F.-G. Levrault, 1827). See, for example, Kurt Jäckel, "Notes sur les sources de la 'Préface de Cromwell,'" *RHLF* 41 (1934): 420–23; and Raymond Schwab, *La Renaissance orientale* (Paris: Payot, 1950), p. 229.

2. *La Préface de Cromwell,* pp. 175–76.

3. Ibid., p. 266. Refer to Jan Kamerbeck, Jr., *Tenants et aboutissants de la notion "couleur locale,"* Utrechtse Publikaties voor Algemene Literatur-wetenschap, no. 2 (Utrecht: Institut voor Algemene Literaturwetenschap, 1962), pp. 31–32.

4. J. Huizinga, *The Waning of the Middle Ages* (New York: Doubleday, An-chor, 1954), p. 242.

5. "Préface," *Histoire des ducs de Bourgogne de la maison de Valois, 1364–1477,* 2nd ed.,24 vols. (Paris: Ladvocat, 1824–1825) 1: iii.

6. Ibid., p. xvi.

7. Ibid., p. xliii.

8. Ibid., p. lxii.

9. Pixérécourt, for example, made Commines a character in his 1814 drama, *Charles le Téméraire, ou le Siège de Nancy* (Paris: Barba, 1814).

10. *Quentin Durward,* Everyman Edition (London: Dent, n.d.), p. 36. Hugo knew the translation by J.-B. Defauconpret, 4 vols. (Paris: C. Gosselin, 1823).

11. Pierre Trahard, *La Jeunesse de Prosper Mérimée (1803–1824)* (Paris: Champion, 1924), pp. 312–15.

12. "Préface," *La Jaquerie,* in *Oeuvres complètes,* ed. Pierre Trahard and Edouard Champion, (Paris: Champion, 1931), 9: 3.

13. Ibid.

14. Ibid., p. 34.

15. *Le Globe* (28 June 1828), p. 503.

16. Ibid., p. 505.

17. *Histoire de France,* vols. 1–7 (Paris: Hachette, 1833–55), 4 (1840): 57.

18. *Histoire de France* (1841), 5: 402.

19. *Histoire de France* (1844), 6: 488–90.

20. The following articles treat the question of the sources Hugo used: Max Bach, "Le Vieux Paris dans *Notre Dame:* Sources et ressources de Victor Hugo," *PMLA* 80 (1965): 321–24; Georges Huard, " 'Notre-Dame de Paris' et les antiquaires de Normandie," *RHLF* 53 (1953): 319–44; Edmond Huguet, "Quelques sources de '*Notre-Dame de Paris,*' *RHLF* 8 (1901): 48–79, 425–55, 622–49; and "Notes sur les sources de *Notre-Dame de Paris,*' " *RHLF* 10 (1903): 287–89. Marius-François Guyard gives detailed notation of the sources of particular passages in his edition of the novel (Paris: Garnier, 1961). Subsequent references in the text will be to Guyard's edition of *Notre-Dame de Paris.*

21. Richard Grant notes that "both the positive and negative aspects of the lower class are captured in *Notre-Dame* by the image of the sea, which makes an early appearance here in Hugo's fiction." *The Perilous Quest,* p. 65. Pierre Halbwachs claims that the royalist myth of a unified medieval society is destroyed in *Notre-Dame.* "Le Poète de l'histoire" in *Oeuvres complètes,* (1968), 7: xxx.

22. See the "Introduction" to this book.

23. "Rêverie d'un passant à propos d'un roi" (May, 1830) *Les Feuilles d'automne* in *Oeuvres poétiques,* 1: 724. The image has its source in Virgil (1345, note 3).

24. In an article by that title in *Le Globe* (8 April 1829), pp. 220–23.

25. Ibid., p. 220.

26. Ibid., p. 221.

27. The article appeared on 30 August 1830; it is discussed by Herbert J. Hunt, *Le Socialisme et le romantisme en France: Etude de la presse socialiste de 1830 à 1848* (Oxford: Clarendon Press, 1935), pp. 42–43.

28. See Hunt, pp. 4–5.

29. Simaïka says that "en se conformant à la conception courante du moyen âge . . . V. Hugo a flatté un goût superficiel qui se retrouve encore aujourd'hui." *L'Inspiration épique dans les romans de Victor Hugo* (Geneva and Paris: Droz and Minard, 1962) p. 52.

30. Thomas Thomov has classified the vocabulary of *Notre-Dame de Paris* to show how Hugo used language to enhance the picturesque in the novel. *Victor Hugo et le moyen âge* (Sofia: Imprimerie de la Cour, 1921), pp. 54–76.

31. Hugo commits an anachronism here; Robert d'Estouteville died in 1479. See Guyard's note, p. 225.

32. The psychological implications of this image are summarized by Grant in *The Perilous Quest*, pp. 51–52, who then sees the whole novel as a working out of the image of the spider and the fly, pp. 53–64.

33. F.P. Kirsch calls the cathedral a magnet. "Die Struktur von Notre-Dame de Paris im Lichte des Kathedralensymbols," *Zeitschrift für Französische Sprache und Literatur,* 78 (1968): 10–34.

34. "Le Moyen Age de Victor Hugo," p. iii.

35. Mallion, *Victor Hugo et l'art architectural,* pp. 61–78.

36. Hugo's essay "Guerre aux démolisseurs" appeared in two versions in 1825 and 1832. Paul Frankl says that Hugo's concern for "historically correct renovation" was a new approach to the gothic. *The Gothic. Literary Sources and Interpretations Through Eight Centuries* (Princeton: Princeton University Press, 1960), p. 484.

37. See my article "The Political Evolution of Victor Hugo's Gothic Vision," pp. 278–79.

38. Paul Zumthor interprets the theme of fatality from the point of view of Hugo's faith in the ability of the written word to recapture the past. "Le Moyen Age de Victor Hugo," p. ii.

39. There are parallels between the aesthetic theory of Hugo in *Notre-Dame de Paris* and that of Hegel. See Mallion, part three, "Le Théoricien de l'architecture," *Victor Hugo et l'art architectural,* passim.

40. Letter to Jules Lechevalier, *Correspondance,* 1: 153–54.

41. "Moi. 1825–1851," *Tas de pierres,* 243–44.

42. C.W. Thompson has indicated Hugo's use of pictorial models, including Rembrandt and Goya, in the novel. *Victor Hugo and the Graphic Arts,* pp. 132–40.

43. *L'Inspiration* p. 54.

44. "Introduction," *Notre-Dame de Paris,* p. xxiv.

45. Revised and reprinted in *Littérature et philosophie mêlées, Oeuvres complètes, Philosophie,* I (1934): 116.

46. See Barrère, *Hugo, l'homme et l'oeuvre,* p. 63.

47. Bibliothèque Nationale, n.a.fr. 13404, fol. 66.

48. *Correspondance,* 2: 330.

49. "Victor Hugo romancier," *Tel Quel,* no. 16 (1964): 61.

50. Ibid., p. 62.

51. Jean Gaudon has made an important observation about the nature of Hugo's imaginative world. "Le monde de Hugo n'est pas conceptuel. C'est le dynamisme propre de la rêverie verbale qui, peu à peu, l'édifie et, par la

continuité et le sérieux de son application, en fait une image cohérente et mouvante de la réalité dans toute sa complexité." *Le Temps,* p. 407.

52. An exception to this type of characterization is the chapter "Fièvre" which provides a psychological study of Frollo's way of viewing the world when under intense emotional pressure.

53. Pierre Albouy's remarks about the characters of *Quatrevingt-treize* are applicable here, also. "La simplification et l'exagération qui accompagnent ce symbolisme, ont pour effet l'immobilité du personnage. Comment changerait-il? Il n'existe que par sa fonction de symbole et pour l'exercer. Et il l'exerce avec une sincérité fanatique." *La Création mythologique,* p. 186.

Chapter 5

1. *Les Burgraves* (Paris: E. Michaud, 1843).

2. *Souvenirs d'un hugolâtre: La génération de 1830* (Paris: J. Lévy, 1885), p. 229.

3. Louis Maigron, *Le Romantisme et la mode* (Paris: Champion, 1911), pp. 1–132. Janine Dakyns points out that while the public was enthusiastic about the Middle Ages in the 1830s, imaginative writers of the first rank evidently felt that medieval themes were exhausted as sources of literary inspiration. *The Middle Ages in French Literature, 1851–1900* (London: Oxford University Press, 1973), pp. 26–27.

4. Quoted by Maigron, ibid., p. 107.

5. *Oeuvres poétiques,* 1: 770.

6. "Je suis fait d'ombre et de marbre" (1854), *Les Quatre Vents de l'esprit, Oeuvres complètes, Poésie,* X (1908): 233.

7. "Contemplation suprême" in *Post-scriptum de ma vie, Oeuvres complètes, Philosophie,* II (1937): 611.

8. *Le Rhin,* p. 341. Barrère gives an analysis of Hugo's poetic vision at Heidelberg in *Hugo, l'homme et l'oeuvre,* p. 101.

9. Jean Gaudon aptly remarks that the Virgilian quality which dominates much of Hugo's poetry in the 1830s disappears in the poem "A Albert Durer," though the change is not permanent at this point in his career. *Le Temps,* pp. 76–77.

10. In addition to the evidence cited in chapter 3, p. 30 and nn. 37 and 38, Hugo also knew Rivarol because there was fleeting reference to him in the "Notes de travail" of the "Reliquat" to "William Shakespeare": "Rivarol: Dante est un cauchemar" (Bibliothèque Nationale, n.a.fr. 24776, fol. 384). Hugo probably used Rivarol's translation in connection with his reading on the art of translation for the introduction to François Victor's version of Shakespeare. For the reference to La Mennais, see *William Shakespeare* in *Oeuvres complètes, Philosophie,* II (1937): 348, hereafter cited as *William Shakespeare.*

11. Antoni Deschamps, trans., *La Divine Comédie de Dante Alighieri* (Paris: Gosselin, 1829), pp. xiii–xiv.

12. Ibid., pp. lvii–lix.

13. Ibid.
14. Quoted by Werner P. Friederich, *Dante's Fame Abroad, 1350–1850* (Rome: Edizioni di Storia e Letteratura, 1950), p. 163.
15. The text is that of the *Oeuvres poétiques,* 1: 991–92.
16. See P. Albouy's discussion in *Oeuvres poétiques,* 1: 1508. Hugo suggests Dante's powers as seer with his description of his piercing eyes in "Ecrit sur un exemplaire de la Divina Commedia" (1843), published in *Les Contemplations,* bk. 3: i.
17. The text is in the *Oeuvres poétiques,* 1: 963–64.
18. *Allemagne devant les lettres françaises de 1814 à 1835,* 2d ed. (Paris: A. Colin, 1965).
19. Paul Berret says that the influence of Germany on Hugo was momentary. *Le Moyen Age dans la Légende des Siècles et les sources de Victor Hugo* (Paris: Paulin, 1911), p. 249. Hugo knew, however, many German romantic works via translation; as well, he praises Beethoven and the German spirit in *William Shakespeare.*
20. Charles Dédéyan, *Victor Hugo et l'Allemagne,* 2 vols. (Paris: Minard, 1964–65), 2: 389. On Hugo and Dürer, see Albouy's note, *Oeuvres poétiques,* 1: 1491–92.
21. *Oeuvres poétiques,* 1: 1104.
22. A summary of Hugo's political career during his preparation of *Les Burgraves* is given by Olga W. Russell in *Etude historique et critique des Burgraves de Victor Hugo* (Paris: Nizet, 1962), pp. 22–28, 83–87.
23. The phrase is used by Elliott M. Grant in *The Career of Victor Hugo* (Cambridge, Mass.: Harvard University Press, 1945), p. 129.
24. Jean Gaudon describes the political situation at the time of Hugo's 1840 trip to Germany in his "Présentation" to *Le Rhin* in the *Oeuvres complètes* (1968), 6: 175–79.
25. "Au bord des flots, au sein des sombres Babylones" (1841) in *Toute la lyre,* I, *Oeuvres complètes, Poésie,* XII (1935): 71.
26. Dédéyan gives an account of this literature in his *Victor Hugo et l'Allemagne,* 2: 396–416.
27. *Le Rhin,* p. 10. Subsequent pagination from *Le Rhin* will be included in the text.
28. Barrère contrasts the actual chronology of Hugo's trips of 1839 and 1840 with the references in *Le Rhin.* The visit to the main part of the Rhine region (Aix-la-Chapelle to Heidelberg in the book) was made in 1840, not in 1838. *La Fantaisie,* 1: 417–21.
29. Hugo's use of his sources is discussed by Dédéyan in *Victor Hugo et L'Allemagne,* 2: 449–87.
30. The phrase is Albouy's in *La Création mythologique,* p. 84.
31. According to the "Historique du Rhin" of the national edition, the following sections were added to the original letters: the legend of the construction of the church at Aix-la-Chapelle, (9), pp. 67–70; "De Lorch à Bingen" (20), pp. 153–84, "La Légende du Beau Pécopin (21), pp. 185–228, "Bingen" (22), pp. 229–38, and "Le Rhin" (25), pp. 262–81. Jean Gaudon in the "Présentation" to *Le Rhin,* p. 175, says that the following were also

added: "Worms-Mannheim" (26), 282–301, "Spire" (27), 302–6, "Schauff-hausen" (37), 394–96, and "La Cataracte du Rhin" (38), 397–401.

32. Jean Mallion gives a résumé of Hugo the antiquarian's treatment of architecture in *Le Rhin* (*Victor Hugo et l'art architectural*, pp. 129-235). I am discussing only the portions of *Le Rhin* in which Hugo gives most of his attention to legend and history as he would develop them in *Les Burgraves*.

33. *Le Rhin*, p. 67. As Hugo adapts Schreiber's legend, he makes some subtle changes which reveal his adeptness as a story teller.

34. According to Dédéyan, this catalogue is based almost entirely on Schreiber. *Victor Hugo et l'Allemagne*, 2: 463–70.

35. Quoted by Karl-Adolpf Knappe in *Albrecht Dürer, The Complete Engravings, Etchings, and Woodcuts* (New York: Abrams, 1965), p. xli. Barrère points out the influence of this engraving on Hugo's view of the *chevalier*, particularly in *La Légende des Siècles* in "Victor Hugo et les arts plastiques," *RLC* 30 (1956): 207. The article is reprinted in Barrère's *Victor Hugo à l'oeuvre* (Paris: Klincksieck, 1965), pp. 247–79.

36. Reproduced in *Victor Hugo dessinateur,* preface by Gaëtan Picon (Paris: Editions du Minotaure, 1963), pp. 56–57.

37. Jean Gaudon emphasizes the wit and skill with which Hugo works the linguistic and geographic details borrowed from Rocales into his text ("Présentation" to *Le Rhin*, pp. 187–88). For a fully developed discussion, consult Jean Giraud, "Victor Hugo et 'Le Monde' de Rocales," *RHLF* 17 (1910): 497–530 and "Victor Hugo et le folklore rhénan. Une source du 'Rhin'," *Revue Germanique,* 7 (1911): 536–57.

38. Gaudon sees affinities between the "Légende," the tradition of Perrault and Nodier and the conventions of La Fontaine ("Présentation," pp. 188–90). Barrère notes parallels between the tale and *Candide (La Fantaisie,* 1: 270–71).

39. "Le Moyen Age de Victor Hugo," pp. xvi–xvii.

40. "Reliquat," *Le Rhin,* p. 495.

41. Dédéyan summarizes Hugo's idea of the history of the Rhine and his use of sources in *Victor Hugo et l'Allemagne*, 2: 499–516.

42. Bibliothèque Nationale, n.a.fr. 24756, fol. 14.

43. There is no precision in Hugo's chronology. The edict of 1356 established that the emperor be elected by seven representatives, four secular and three ecclesiastical. Hugo speaks of only four secular electors here (p. 118), but mentions the archbishops of Cologne, Mainz, and Trier later (p. 119). In letter 25, he describes the process of electing the emperor (pp. 272–75).

44. In letter 27 Hugo describes the cathedral of Spire where many emperors were buried and takes up again the theme that death separates the man from the power of the emperorship but also accords him new grandeur (p. 305).

45. "Monographie historique du Rhin," Bibliothèque Nationale, n.a.fr. 24756, fol. 35.

Chapter 6

1. *Théâtre complet,* notices and notes by J.-J. Thierry et Josette Mélèze, Pléiade Edition, 2 vols. (Paris: Gallimard, 1964), 2: 15; subsequent pagination given in the text will be from this edition.
2. Jean Gaudon, *Hugo dramaturge* (Paris: L'Arche, 1955), p. 18.
3. *Les Rayons et les ombres* in *Oeuvres poétiques,* 1: 1030–31. Fernand Baldensperger has shown how closely *Les Burgraves* follows the themes and techniques of the Romantic theater and notes that the use of the Middle Ages may well derive from Hugo's nonliterary ambitions. "Les Grands Thèmes romantiques dans les *Burgraves* de Victor Hugo," *Archiv für das Studium der neueren Sprachen und Literaturen,* 121 (1908): 391–410.
4. Albouy, *La Création mythologique,* pp. 265–67. Massin gives a schematic presentation of parallels between *Hernani* and *Les Burgraves* in his "Présentation" to *Les Burgraves* in the *Oeuvres complètes* (1968), 6: 558.
5. See Albouy, *La Création mythologique,* p. 267.
6. Ibid., p. 70.
7. Russell comments that Hugo "exprime une sorte de mal du siècle approfondi, enrichi, et animé par son expérience personnelle." *Etude historique,* p. 93.
8. Bibliothèque Nationale, n.a.fr. 13374, fol. 8.
9. *Hugo, l'homme et l'oeuvre,* p. 107.
10. "Les Grands Thèmes romantiques dans les *Burgraves,*" pp. 392, 410.
11. *Etude historique,* p. 220.
12. "Le Moyen Age de Victor Hugo," p. xix. Hugo states in the preface that he wishes to situate the action in the three areas of the *burg:* fortress, palace, and cavern. The manuscript shows his sketch for the setting of part one; this in itself indicates his concern that medieval décor reinforce the thematic development of the play.
13. "Le Moyen Age de Victor Hugo," p. xix.
14. Discussions of the relationship between Hugo's theater and melodrama are given by Gaudon, *Hugo dramaturge,* passim, and Michel Butor, "Le Théâtre de Victor Hugo," (part two) *NRF* 12 (1964): 1073–81.
15. "Le Théâtre de Victor Hugo," (part one), *NRF* 12 (1964): 864.
16. Ibid., pp. 864–78.
17. Ibid., pp. 867–68.
18. The legends regarding Barbarossa are drawn largely from Aloys Schreiber's *Traditions populaires du Rhin,* 2 vols. (Heidelberg: J. Englemann, 1830–31).
19. *Etude historique,* p. 113.

Chapter 7

1. *Oeuvres complètes, Histoire,* I (1907): 20.
2. Ibid., p. 168.
3. Ibid., p. 190.
4. Ibid.
5. *Histoire du romantisme* (Paris: Charpentier, 1874), p. 127.

6. See Counson, *Dante en France,* pp. 191–92 and Friederich *Dante's Fame Abroad,* p. 170.

7. ll. 415–20. The text is from Paul Berret's edition (Paris: Hachette, 1932), 1: 45.

8. *William Shakespeare,* pp. 38–39.

9. *Oeuvres complètes, Poésie,* IX (1927): 108.

10. Hugo repeats an impression first expressed in "Ecrit sur la première page d'un Pétrarque" in 1835 *(Les Chants du crépuscule).*

11. A post-exile letter (18 July 1874) to the committee constituted at Avignon on the occasion of the five-hundredth anniversary of the death of Petrarch. *Oeuvres complètes, Actes et Paroles,* III (1940): 207–8.

12. This letter is discussed in detail by Francesco Siccardo in "Dante e Victor Hugo," *RLC* 39 (1965): 427–33.

13. Perhaps there is an echo here of Frédéric Ozanam's *Dante et la philosophie catholique au treizième siècle* (Paris: Périsse frères, 1839). In his introduction to the first edition, Ozanam states: "Or, voici une philosophie qui s'exprime dans la langue la plus mélodieuse de l'Europe," p. 9.

14. Reprinted by Siccardo, p. 432. An emphasis on Dante as the visionary who can see truth and knowledge in advance is also found, for example, in *L'Ane* (Pt. VI. "Conduite de l'homme vis-à-vis des génies") in the edition by Pierre Albouy (Paris: Flammarion, 1966), ll. 1331–43.

15. *William Shakespeare,* p. 37.

16. Ibid., p. 38.

17. Ibid., p. 44.

18. Numerous parallels between Hugo and Michelet have been pointed out. See Jean-Marie Carré, "Victor Hugo et Michelet," *Revue de France,* 4 (1924): 722–35. Dakyns dates Michelet's attacks on the Middle Ages from 1845. *The Middle Ages in French Literature,* p. 49. On views of the Middle Ages during the Second Empire, see pp. 110–91.

19. On the significance of Michelet's concept of the Renaissance, see Wallace K. Ferguson, *The Renaissance in Historical Thought* (Boston: Houghton Mifflin, 1948), pp. 173–78. On the influence of Vico, Herder, Quinet, and Cousin on Michelet, consult Gustave Lanson, "La Formation de la méthode historique de Michelet," *Revue d'histoire moderne et contemporaine,* 7 (1905–6): 5–31.

20. "Introduction," *Histoire de France* (1855), 7: iv.

21. Ibid., p. ix.

22. Ibid., p. clv.

23. Ibid., pp. clvii–clix.

24. Hugo was never attracted by the figure of Jeanne d'Arc as was Michelet, although she was viewed as a heroic figure by the latter. After exile, Hugo refers to her as a visionary *(Travailleurs de la Mer,* pt. I, ch. I, p. 7) and as a radiant martyr ("Les Malheureux," ll. 86–88, *Les Contemplations).*

25. *Les Misérables,* ed. Marius-François Guyard, 2 vols. (Paris: Garner, 1957), 2: 526. See also my article, "The Political Evolution of Victor Hugo's Gothic Vision," passim.

26. *Les Misérables,* 1: 756.

27. Ibid., 2: 42.

28. Ibid., 2: 207.
29. "Promontorium somnii" in *William Shakespeare*, p. 317.
30. Ibid.
31. Ibid.
32. Ibid., p. 318.
33. Ibid. A dazzling list of names follows which is taken from sources such as Collin de Plancy, Schreiber, and Shakespeare. See the notes of the Journet-Robert edition of *Promontorium somnii,* eds. R. Journet and G. Robert (Paris: Les Belles Lettres, 1961), pp. 128–37.
34. Ibid., p. 320.
35. From chapter 2, "Pourquoi le moyen âge désespéra" in *La Sorcière,* chronology and preface by Paul Viallaneix (Paris: Garnier-Flammarion, 1966), p. 60.
36. See the Journet-Robert edition of *Promontorium somnii,* pp. 289–301.
37. *William Shakespeare*, p. 44. Hugo also states that Cervantes and Rabelais close the Middle Ages.
38. François-Victor Hugo, "Introduction," *Oeuvres complètes de W. Shakespeare,* 18 vols. (Paris: Pagnerre, 1859–1866), 2: 8.
39. Ibid., p. 44.
40. See chaps. 3 and 4, passim.
41. As in "La Pente de la rêverie" (1830), *Oeuvres poétiques,* 1: 770.
42. *Oeuvres complètes, Roman,* VIII (1907): 31, 333. *Gothique* as a synonym for *médiéval* is not always pejorative. In *Les Travailleurs de la mer,* Hugo suggests the solitude of Gilliatt's work to salvage the wrecked steamboat by a comparison with the Middle Ages: "Le charpentier gothique avait un aide, son fils; Gilliatt était seul." *Oeuvres complètes, Roman,* VII (1911): 290.
43. Onzième fragment, "Les Voix" of *Dieu;* the text is from *La Légende des Siècles, La Fin de Satan, Dieu,* ed. J. Truchet (Paris: Gallimard, 1950), p. 969.
44. *Les Quatre Vents de l'esprit* in *Oeuvres complètes, Poésie,* X (1908): 95.
45. Maurice Lange, "Victor Hugo et les sources de 'La Vision de Dante,' " *RHLF* 25 (1918): 548.
46. The text is from the Truchet edition, p. 663; all subsequent pagination is from this Pléiade edition.
47. "La Vision d'où est sorti ce livre," pp. 8, 11.

Chapter 8

1. *Oeuvres complètes,* ed. F.-F. Gautier (Paris: Nouvelle Revue Française, 1923), 4: 135.
2. The terms are those of C.S. Lewis in *A Preface to Paradise Lost* (1942; rpt. New York: Oxford University Press, Galaxy, 1961).
3. *The Epic in Nineteenth-Century France* (Oxford: Blackwell, 1941), passim.
4. *William Shakespeare*, p. 46.
5. Berret discusses in detail Hugo's use of Jubinal in *Le Moyen Age,* pp. 32–39 and 43–59.

6. *La Légende des Siècles, La Fin de Satan, Dieu,* p. 3; subsequent pagination given in the text will be from Truchet's Pléiade edition.

7. Paul Zumthor, *Victor Hugo poète de Satan,* 7th ed. (Paris: Robert Laffont, 1946), p. 98.

8. "La Trompette du jugement," p. 736, "Abîme," p. 740.

9. Zumthor, *Victor Hugo pòte de Satan,* p. 73.

10. *Correspondance,* 2: 188.

11. Berret stresses the influence of the doctrines of Saint-Simon and Fourier on Hugo from 1854–1859 in *La Philosophie de Victor Hugo en 1854–1859* (Paris: Paulin, 1910).

12. "L'Amour," *Légende,* p. 530.

13. A thesis of Zumthor's *Victor Hugo poète de Satan* is that *La Fin de Satan* is the poem of revolution.

14. "L'Amour," p. 527. This poem appeared in the "série complémentaire" of the *Légende.*

15. *Hugo, l'homme et l'oeuvre,* p. 165.

16. Alfred Glauser, *Hugo et la poésie pure* (Geneva and Paris: Droz and Minard, 1957), p. 88.

17. Charles Baudouin, "Le Thème du héros dans la *Légende des Siècles," Action et pensée* 27 (1951): 72.

18. Paul Zumthor uses the phrase in "Le Moyen Age de Victor Hugo," p. xxviii.

19. The Renaissance did not result in the complete liberation of man. In the first series, "Le Satyre" is followed by "La Rose de l'Infante" and "L'Inquisition. Les Raisons du Momotombo" which indict sixteenth-century Spain.

20. Berret notes that, in using the term *paladin,* Hugo was inspired by the Round Table. See *La Légende des Siècles,* ed. Paul Berret, 6 vols. (Paris: Hachette, 1921–27), 1: 237–39.

21. Zumthor, *Victor Hugo poète de Satan,* p. 101.

22. pp. 5-6. .

23. Baudouin, "Le Thème du héros," p. 71.

24. *Le Moyen Age,* p. 387.

25. Ibid., p. 388.

26. Jubinal's text and Hugo's text are compared by Berret in *Le Moyen Age,* pp. 32–37.

27. Berret, Ibid., p. 38.

28. Ibid., pp. 43–64.

29. In another poem, "Le Campéador, l'homme honnête et sans ennui," the Cid is described as "terrible et doux, cher à l'Espagne." *Toute la lyre,* I, 16 in *Oeuvres complètes, Poésie,* XII (1935): 39.

30. *Le Moyen Age,* p. 99.

31. Hugo uses a similar technique in "Bivar." A sheik, coming to visit the Cid in exile, is astonished to find that he seems to have none of the trappings of a hero. After many words by the visitor, the Cid makes two laconic remarks which terminate the poem.

32. Hugo also uses his memories of the Spanish countryside in depicting the destruction and suffering caused by misrule in "Le Jour des Rois."

33. *Le Moyen Age,* pp. 135–52, 259–63. Berret suggests that Hugo may have been inspired by the legend, "L'Abbé de Saint-Victor," in *Légendes françaises* of Edouard d'Anglemont (1829).

34. Jacques Truchet's note in the *Légende,* p. 1175.

35. Paul Zumthor views "Eviradnus" as the embodiment of the Hugolian Middle Ages. "Le vocabulaire typique atteint alors son expansion maximum, et un haut degré d'organisation. Il embrasse plusieurs dizaines de mots-clés, combinables en centaines de formules" ("Le Moyen Age de Victor Hugo," p. xxiii). Zumthor then discusses the complex patterns of imagery in the poem, beginning with the basic opposition of *noir-lumineux* (pp. xxiii-xxv).

36. See Glauser, *Hugo et la poésie pure,* p. 89.

37. The first version of "Welf"—"Le Vieux de Brisach"—is published in *Toute la lyre,* I, 19 in *Oeuvres complètes, Poésie,* XII (1935): 42–43, and is dated 1858–59. Originally scheduled for publication as part of the *Théâtre en liberté,* "Welf" is paralleled by *L'Epée,* another drama recreating the atmosphere of *Les Burgraves.*

38. Hugo treats the problems of pardon and of expiation and punishment in the "Sultan Mourad" and "Le Parricide" (1858).

39. *Le Moyen Age,* pp. 330–63.

Chapter 9

1. *Notre-Dame de Paris,* p. 567.

2. Ibid., p. 568.

3. See *Victor Hugo dessinateur,* no. 62, p. 67.

4. "Ecrit en 1846," ll. 231–44, *Les Contemplations,* V, iii.

5. *Légende,* p. 113.

6. *Les Quatre Vents de l'esprit, Oeuvres complètes, Poésie,* X (1908): 110. Hugo's dislike of the gallows is paralleled by his portrait of the fifteenth-century inquisitor Torquemada, who is the subject of his drama, written in 1869 and published in 1882. The play has no medieval atmosphere, and Hugo portrays Torquemada as a mistaken visionary whose unbending dogmas lead in the end to the destruction of Don Sanche and Doña Rose, who had saved his life earlier.

7. Ibid., pp. 148–49.

8. *Toute la lyre,* VIII, 3 in *Oeuvres complètes, Poésie,* XII (1935): 307. Hugo's use of pejorative allusions to the Middle Ages in the 1870s is in contrast with the generally positive interest in the period which was part of the national regeneration of the post-1870 period. See Dakyns, *The Middle Ages in French Literature,* pp. 195–205, expecially p. 201.

9. See the "Introduction." pp. 1f.

10. *Les Quatre Vents de l'esprit,* pp. 76–77.

11. Cf. Georg Lukács's discussion of Scott in *The Historical Novel,* trans. Hannah Mitchell and Stanley Mitchell (Boston: Beacon, 1963), pp. 30–63.

12. *Quatrevingt-treize,* prepared by Jean Boudout (Paris: Garnier, 1957), p. 219; all subsequent pagination given in the text will be from this edition.

13. *La Gaule poétique*, 1: 81.

14. The complete description of the tower is given on pp. 292–306.

15. Etienne Aubrée, *Victor Hugo et Juliette Drouet à Fougères*, new edition (Paris: Perrin, 1942). A comparison of the sketches of the château at Fougères (1836) and La Tourgue (1876) illustrates how Hugo retained and transformed these mental pictures. See *Victor Hugo dessinateur*, no. 16, p. 49 and no. 365, p. 232.

16. Jean Delalande, *Victor Hugo à Hauteville-House* (Paris: Albin Michel, 1947).

Selected Bibliography

Manuscript Sources

Hugo, Victor. Bibliothèque Nationale. Nouvelles acquisitions françaises: "Les Burgraves," 13374; "Carnets," 13441–13445; "Cromwell," 13667; "En Voyage," 13391; "Légende des Siècles," Première série, 24736; "Légende des Siècles," Nouvelle série, 24757; "Légende des Siècles, Reliquat," 24775; "Notre-Dame de Paris," 13378; "Notre-Dame de Paris, Correspondance," 13404; "Odes et Ballades," 13393; "Le Rhin," 13387; "Le Rhin. Reliquat et documents," 24756; "William Shakespeare," 13366," "William Shakespeare, Reliquat et documents," 24776.

Printed Sources

Editions of Hugo's Works

L'Ane. Edited by Pierre Albouy. Paris: Flammarion, 1966.

Les Burgraves. Paris: E. Michaud, 1843.

Carnet (mars-avril 1856). Edited by R. Journet and G. Robert. Paris: Les Bélles-Lettres, 1959.

Les Châtiments. New edition by Paul Berret. 2 vols. Paris: Hachette, 1932.

Choses vues, 1830–1854. Notices and notes by Paul Sauchon. Reprint. Paris: Plon, 1962.

Les Contemplations. Edited by Joseph Vianey. New edition. 3 vols. Paris: Hachette, 1922.

Les Contemplations. Edited by Jacques Seebacher. 2 vols. Paris: A. Colin, 1964.

Correspondance: 1815–1882. 2 vols. Paris: Calmann-Levy, 1896–1898.

Journal (1830–1848). Presented by Henri Guillemin. Paris: Gallimard, 1954.

La Légende des Siècles. Edited by Paul Berret. 6 vols. Paris: Hachette, 1921–1927.

La Légende des Siècles, La Fin de Satan, Dieu. Edited by J. Truchet. Pléiade Edition. Paris: Gallimard, 1950.

Les Misérables. Edited by Marius-François Guyard. 2 vols. Paris: Garnier, 1957.

Notre-Dame de Paris. Edited by Marius-François Guyard. Paris: Garnier, 1961.

Oeuvres complètes. 45 vols. Paris: Ollendorff, Albin Michel, 1904–1952.

Oeuvres complètes. Chronological edition, edited by Jean Massin. 18 vols. Paris: Club français du livre, 1967–1970.

Oeuvres poétiques. Edited by Pierre Albouy. Pléiade Edition. 2 vols. Paris: Gallimard, 1964 and 1967.

Pierres (vers et prose). Edited by Henri Guillemin. Geneva: Milieu du Monde, 1951.

La Préface de Cromwell. Edited by Maurice Souriau. Paris: Boivin, 1897.

Promontorium somnii. Edited by R. Journet and G. Robert. Paris: Les Belles-Lettres, 1961.

Quatrevingt-treize. Prepared by Jean Boudout. Paris: Garnier, 1957.

Théâtre complet. Notices and notes by J.-J. Thierry and Josette Mélèze. 2 vols. Pléiade Edition. Paris: Gallimard, 1964.

Trois albums. Edited by R. Journet and G. Robert. Paris: Les Belles-Lettres, 1963.

Victor Hugo dessinateur. Preface by Gaëtan Picon, notes by Roger Cornaille and Georges Herscher. Paris: Editions du Minotaure, 1963.

Pertinent Texts and Translations

Ampère, Jean-Jacques Antoine. *La Grèce, Rome et Dante: Etudes littéraires d'après nature.* Paris: Didier, 1848.

[Balzac, Honoré de.] *Clotilde de Lusignan.* 4 vols. Paris: Hubert, 1822.

Barante, Guillaume, Baron de. *Histoire des ducs de Bourgogne de la maison de Valois, 1364–1477.* 2d ed. 24 vols. Paris: Ladvocat, 1824–25.

Beckford, William. *Vathek.* Paris: Poinçot, 1787.

Catalogue sommaire d'un bon MOBILIER. Paris: Maulde et Renou, 1852.

Chateaubriand, François-René de. *Génie du Christianisme.* Chronology and introduction by Pierre Reboul. 2 vols. Paris: Garnier-Flammarion, 1966.

Collin de Plancy. *Dictionnaire infernal.* 2d ed. 4 vols. Paris: P. Mongie aîné, 1825–26.

Creuzer, Frédéric. *Religions de l'antiquité, considérées principalement dans leurs formes symboliques et mythologiques.* Translated by J.-D. Guigniaut. 10 vols. Paris: Treuttel et Würtz, 1825–51.

Deschamps, Antoni, trans. *La Divine Comédie de Dante Alighieri.* Paris: Gosselin, 1829.

Dumas, Alexandre, père. *Oeuvres complètes. Théâtre.* 6 vols. Paris: Charpentier, 1834–36.

Dürer, Albrecht, The Complete Engravings, Etchings, and Woodcuts. Text by Karl-Adolpf Knapp. New York: Abrams, 1965.

Fauriel, Claude-Charles. *Dante et les origines de la langue et de la littérature italienne.* 2 vols. Paris: A. Durand, 1854.

Herder, Johann G. von. *Idées sur la philosophie de l'histoire de l'humanité.* Translated by E. Quinet. 3 vols. Paris: F.-G. Levrault, 1827.

Hugo, Abel, trans. *Romances historiques.* Paris: Pélicier, 1822.

Hugo, François-Victor, trans. *Oeuvres complètes de W. Shakespeare.* 18 vols. Paris: Pagnerre, 1859–86.

Lewis, Matthew Gregory. *Le Moine.* 2 vols. Paris: Maradan, 1799.

Marchangy, Louis-Antoine-Francois de. *La Gaule poétique.* 3d ed. 8 vols. Paris: C.-F. Patris, 1819.

Maturin, Charles Robert. *Bertram.* Translated by MM. Taylor and Ch. Nodier. Paris: Gide fils et Ladvocat, 1821.

Mérimée, Prosper. *La Jaquerie. Oeuvres complètes.* Vol. 9. Paris: Champion, 1931.

Millevoye, Charles Hubert. *Oeuvres.* Preceded by a notice by M. Sainte-Beuve. Paris: Garnier, 1865.

Nerval, Gérard de, trans. "Poésies allemandes." Vol. 1. *Oeuvres complètes.* Paris: Calmann Levy, 1883.

Nodier, Charles. *Oeuvres complètes.* 13 vols. Paris: Renduel, 1832–37.

Ozanam, Frédéric. *Dante et la philosophie catholique au treizième siècle.* Paris: Périsse frères, 1839.

Pixérécourt, René-Charles Guilbert de. *Charles le Téméraire, ou le Siège de Nancy.* Paris: Barba, 1814.

Rivarol, Antoine de, trans. *L'Enfer, poème du Dante.* 2 vols. Paris: P.-F. Didot le jeune, 1785.

[Sainte-Palaye, La Curne de.] *Histoire littéraire des troubadours.* 3 vols. Published by C.-F.-X. Millot. Paris: Durand, 1774.

————. *Mémoires sur l'ancienne chevalerie.* New edition. 3 vols. Paris: La Veuve Duchesne, 1781.

Schlegel, August Wilhelm von. *Cours de littérature dramatique.* Translated by Mme. Necker de Saussure. 3 vols. Paris and Geneva: Paschaud, 1814.

Schlegel, Friedrich von. *Histoire de la littérature ancienne et moderne.* Translated by William Duckett. 2 vols. Paris: Baltimore, 1829.

Scott, Sir Walter. *Quentin Durward.* Translated by J.-B. Defauconpret. 4 vols. Paris: Gosselin, 1823.

————. *Quentin Durward.* London: Dent, n.d.

Scribe, Eugène, and Delavigne, Germain. *Robert-le-Diable.* Paris: Bezon, 1831.

Staël, Anne-Louise-Germaine, Mme. de. *Corinne ou l'Italie.* Paris: Didot, n.d.

————. *De l'Allemagne.* 2d ed. 3 vols. Paris: H. Nicolle, 1814.

Tressan, Louis, le Comte de. *Oeuvres.* 10 vols. Paris: Nepveu, 1822–23.

Villemain, Abel. *Tableau de la littérature au Moyen Age, en France, en Italie, en Espagne et en Angleterre.* New Edition. 2 vols. Paris: Didier, 1856.

Periodicals

Annales de la littérature et des arts, 1820–23.
Le Catholique, 1826–29.
Le Conservateur littéraire. Edited by J. Marsan. 2 vols. Paris: Hachette, 1922.
Le Drapeau Blanc, 1824–26.
Le Globe, 1828–29.
La Muse française 1823–1824. Edited by J. Marsan. 2 vols. Paris: Cornély, 1907–9.

History and Historiography

Bury, J.B. *The Idea of Progress.* 1932. Reprint. New York: Dover, 1955.
Carré, Jean-Marie. *Michelet et son temps.* 3d ed. Paris: Perrin, 1926.
Collingwood, R.G. *The Idea of History.* 1946. Reprint. New York: Oxford University Press, 1956.

Comines, Philippe de. *Mémoires,* new edition . . . augmented by M. l'Abbé Lenglet du Fresnoy. 4 vols. Paris: Rollin fils, 1747.

Du Breul, Dom Jacques. *Le Théâtre des antiquités de Paris.* Paris: Claude de La Tour, 1612.

Ferguson, Wallace K. *The Renaissance in Historical Thought.* Boston: Houghton Mifflin, 1948.

Huizinga, J. *The Waning of the Middle Ages.* 1949. Reprint. New York: Doubleday, Anchor, 1954.

Kohlrausch, Heinrich. *Histoire d'Allemagne depuis les temps les plus reculés jusqu'à l'année 1838.* 2 vols. Paris: Debicourt, 1838.

Lanson, Gustave. "La Formation de la méthode historique de Michelet."*Revue d'histoire moderne et contemporaine* 7 (1905–6): 5–31.

Mallet, Paul Henri. *Histoire de Danemarc.* 4 vols. Copenhagen: Phillibert, 1758.

Mathieu, Pierre. *Histoire de Louis XI, roi de France.* Paris: P. Mettoyer, 1610.

Meinecke, Friedrich. *Historism: The Rise of a New Historical Outlook.* Translated by J.E. Anderson. New York: Herder and Herder, 1972.

Michelet, Jules. *Histoire de France.* Vols. 1–7. Paris: Hachette, 1833–55.

_____, trans. *Principes de la philosophie de l'histoire.* Translated from la Scienza Nuova of J.B. Vico. Paris: J. Renouard, 1827.

_____. *La Sorcière.* Chronology and preface by Paul Viallaneix. Paris: Garnier-Flammarion, 1966.

Moréri, Louis. *Le Grand Dictionnaire historique.* New edition. 10 vols. Paris: Les Libraires associés, 1759.

Pfeffel von Kriegelstein, Christian Friedrich. *Abrégé chronologique de l'histoire et du droit public d'Allemagne.* 2d ed. Mannheim: Imprimerie électorale, 1758.

Sauval, Henri. *Histoire et recherches des antiquités de la ville de Paris.* 3 vols. Paris: Moette et Chardon, 1724.

Schlegel, Friedrich von. *Philosophie de l'histoire.* Translated by M. l'abbé Lechat. Paris: Parent-Desbarres, 1836.

Schreiber, Aloys, ed. *Traditions populaires du Rhin.* 2 vols. Heidelberg: J. Englemann, 1830–31.

Monographs on Hugo

Albouy, Pierre. *La Création mythologique chez Victor Hugo.* Paris: J. Corti, 1964.

Aubrée, Etienne. *Victor Hugo et Juliette Drouet à Fougères.* New edition. Paris: Perrin, 1942.

Barrère, Jean-Bertrand. *La Fantaisie de Victor Hugo.* 3 vols. Paris: Corti, 1949–60.

_____. *Hugo, l'homme et l'oeuvre.* New edition. Paris: Hatier, 1959.

_____. *Victor Hugo à l'oeuvre.* Paris: Klincksieck, 1965.

Bauer, Henri François. *Les Ballades de Victor Hugo: Leurs origines françaises et étrangères.* Paris: Champion, 1936.

Bellessort, André. *Victor Hugo.* 4th ed. Paris: Perrin, 1930.

Berret, Paul. *Le Moyen Age dans La Légende des Siècles et les sources de Victor Hugo.* Paris: Paulin, 1911.

_____. *La Philosophie de Victor Hugo en 1854–1859 et deux mythes de la Légende des Siècles.* Paris: Paulin, 1910.

Brunetière, Ferdinand. *Victor Hugo.* 2d ed. 2 vols. Paris: Hachette, 1906.

Dédéyan, Charles. *Victor Hugo et l'Allemagne.* 2 vols. Paris: Minard, 1964–65.

Delalande, Jean. *Victor Hugo à Hauteville-House.* Paris: Albin Michel, 1947.

Emery, Léon. *Vision et pensée chez Victor Hugo.* Lyon: Audin, [1939].

Gaudon, Jean. *Hugo dramaturge.* Paris: L'Arche, 1955.

_____. *Le Temps de la contemplation.* Paris: Flammarion, 1969.

Glauser, Alfred. *Hugo et la poésie pure.* Geneva and Paris: Droz and Minard, 1957.

Grant, Elliott M. *The Career of Victor Hugo.* Cambridge: Harvard University Press, 1945.

Grant, Richard B. *Perilous Quest: Image, Myth and Prophecy in the Narratives of Victor Hugo.* Durham: Duke University Press, 1968.

Guillemin, Henri. *Victor Hugo par lui-même.* Paris: Seuil, 1951.

Hugo, Adèle. *Victor Hugo raconté par un témoin de sa vie.* 2 vols. Paris: A. Lacroix, 1863.

Journet, René and Guy Robert. *Notes sur les Contemplations,* followed by an index. Paris: Les Belles Lettres, 1958.

Joussain, André. *L'Esthétique de Victor Hugo.* Paris: Boivin, 1920.

Levaillant, M. *La Crise mystique de Victor Hugo.* Paris: J. Corti, 1954.

Mabilleau, Léopold. *Victor Hugo.* Paris: Hachette, 1893.

Mallion, Jean. *Victor Hugo et l'art architectural.* Grenoble: Allier, 1962.

Maurois, André. *Olympio ou la vie de Victor Hugo.* Paris: Hachette, 1954.

O'Connor, Sister M. Irene. *A Study of the Sources of Han d'Islande and Their Significance in the Literary Development of Victor Hugo.* Washington, D.C.: Catholic University of America Press, 1942.

Piroué, Georges. *Victor Hugo romancier.* Paris: Denoël, 1964.

Py, Albert. *Les Mythes grecs dans la poésie de Victor Hugo.* Geneva and Paris: Droz and Minard, 1963.

Renouvier, Charles. *Victor Hugo le philosophe.* Paris: A. Colin, 1900.

_____. *Victor Hugo le poète.* 2d ed. Paris: A. Colin, 1897.

Roos, J. *Les Idées philosophiques de Victor Hugo.* Paris: Nizet, 1958.

Rudwin, Maximilien. *Satan et le satanisme dans l'oeuvre de Victor Hugo.* Paris: Les Belles Lettres, 1926.

Russell, Olga W. *Etude historique et critique des Burgraves de Victor Hugo.* Paris: Nizet, 1962.

Schenck, Eunice Morgan. *La Part de Charles Nodier dans la formation des idées romantiques de Victor Hugo jusqu'à la Préface de Cromwell.* Paris: Champion, 1914.

Sergent, Jean. *Dessins de Victor Hugo.* Geneva: La Palatine, 1955.

Simaïka, Raouf. *L'Inspiration épique dans les romans de Victor Hugo.* Geneva and Paris: Droz and Minard, 1962.

Thomov, Thomas S. *Etude sur la langue et le style de Victor Hugo dans la Légende des Siècles.* Sofia: L'Artiste, 1928.

_____. *Victor Hugo et le moyen âge.* Sofia: Imprimerie de la Cour, 1921.

Thompson, C.W. *Victor Hugo and the Graphic Arts (1820–1833).* Geneva and Paris: Droz, 1970.

Turner, Robert F. *The Sixteenth Century in Victor Hugo's Inspiration.* New York: Columbia University Press, 1934.

Venzac, Géraud. *Les Origines religieuses de Victor Hugo.* Paris: Blaud et Gay, 1955.

_____. *Les Premiers Maîtres de Victor Hugo.* Paris: Blaud et Gay, 1955.

Zumthor, Paul. *Victor Hugo poète de Satan.* 7th ed. Paris: R. Laffont, 1946.

Articles and Essays on Hugo

Albouy, Pierre. "Aux commencements de *La Légende des Siècles.*" *RHLF* 62 (1962): 565–72.

Bach, Max. "First Reactions to Victor Hugo's *Notre-Dame de Paris.*" *Kentucky Foreign Language Quarterly* 3 (1956): 59–66.

_____. "Le Vieux Paris dans *Notre-Dame:* Sources et ressources de Victor Hugo." *PMLA* 80 (1965): 321–24.

Baldensperger, Fernand. "Les Grands Thèmes romantiques dans les *Burgraves* de Victor Hugo." *Archiv für das Studium der neueren Sprachen und Literaturen* 121 (1908): 391–410.

Barrère, Jean-Bertrand. "Les Livres de Hauteville-House." *RHLF* 51 (1951): 441–55; 52 (1952): 48–72.

_____. "Victor Hugo et les arts plastiques." *RLC* 30 (1956): 180–208.

Baudelaire, Charles. "Réflexions" and "Les Misérables" in *L'Art romantique. Oeuvres complètes,* ed. F.-F. Gautier. Vol. 4. Paris: Nouvelle Revue française, 1923.

Baudouin, Charles. "Le Thème du héros dans la *Légende des Siècles.*" *Action et pensée* 27 (1951): 65–79.

Benedetto, Luigi. "Victor Hugo e Dante." *Lettere Italiane* 20 (1968): 40–55.

Berret, Paul. "Guanhumara dans *Les Burgraves.*" *Bulletin de l'Université de Lille,* 2d ser., 6 (1902): 137–43.

Butor, Michel. "Le Théâtre de Victor Hugo." *NRF* 12 (1964): 862–78, 1073–81; 13 (1965): 105–13.

_____. "Victor Hugo critique." *Critique* 21 (1965): 803–26.

_____. "Victor Hugo romancier." *Tel Quel,* no. 16 (1964): 60–77.

Carré, Jean-Marie. "Victor Hugo et Michelet." *Revue de France* 4 (1924): 722–35.

Charles, Paul. "Charles Nodier et Victor Hugo." *RHLF* 39 (1932): 568–86.

Chassé, Charles. "Victor Hugo, Dumas père et le tombeau de Charlemagne à Aix-la-Chapelle." *RSH,* no. 95 (1959): 331–34.

Defaux, G. "Renaissance poétique nationale et influences allemandes dans les *Odes et Ballades.*" *Revue de l'Université d'Ottawa* 41 (1971): 5–24.

Gaudon, Jean. "Notes sur *Le Rhin* de Victor Hugo." *Travaux de linguistique et de littérature* 2 (1964): 31–65.

Georgel, Pierre. "Vision et imagination plastique dans *Quatre-vingt-treize.*" *Lettres romanes* 19 (1965): 3–27.

Girard, René. "Monstres et demi-dieux dans l'oeuvre de Hugo." *Symposium* 19 (1965): 50–57.

Giraud, Jean. "Etude sur quelques sources des *Burgraves.*" *RHLF* 16 (1909): 501–39.

_____. "Une source inconnue du *Rhin* de Victor Hugo: *Les Estats, empires et principautz de Pierre Davity.*" *RHLF* 29 (1922): 165–91.

———. "Victor Hugo et le folklore rhénan. Une source du *'Rhin.'* " *Revue Germanique* 7 (1911): 536–57.

———. "Victor Hugo et 'Le Monde' de Rocales." *RHLF* 17 (1910): 497–530.

Huard, Georges. *"Notre Dame de Paris* et les antiquaires de Normandie." *RHLF* 53 (1953): 319–44.

Huguet, Edmond. "Notes sur les sources de *Notre-Dame de Paris." RHLF* 10 (1903): 287–89.

———. "Quelques sources de *Notre-Dame de Paris." RHLF* 8 (1901): 48–79, 425–55, 622–49.

Jäckel, Kurt. "Notes sur les sources de la 'Préface de Cromwell.' " *RHLF* 41 (1934): 420–23.

Kirsch, Fritz Peter. "Die Struktur von Notre-Dame de Paris im Lichte des Kathedralensymbols." *Zeitschrift für Französische Sprache und Literatur* 78 (1968): 10–34.

Lange, Maurice. "Victor Hugo et les sources de 'La vision de Dante.' " *RHLF* 25 (1918): 532–61.

Larroutis, M. "J. de Maistre et V. Hugo: le bourreau dans Han d'Islande." *RHLF* 62 (1962): 573–75.

Péès, Simone. "L'Origine de la couleur locale scandinave dans le 'Han d'Islande' de Victor Hugo." *RLC* 9 (1929): 261–84.

Refort, Lucien. "L'Art gothique vu par Victor Hugo et Michelet." *RHLF* 33 (1926): 390–94.

Richard, Jean-Pierre. "Paysage et langage chez Hugo." *Critique* 25 (1969): 387–407.

Riffaterre, Michael. "Victor Hugo, Critic of Shakespeare." *The American Society Legion of Honor Magazine* 31 (1960): 139–52.

———. "Victor Hugo's Poetics." *The American Society Legion of Honor Magazine* 32 (1961): 181–96.

———. "La Vision hallucinatoire chez Victor Hugo." *MLN* 78 (1963): 225–41. Reprinted in *Essais de stylistique structurale.* Translated by Daniel Delas. Paris: Flammarion, 1971.

Sergent, Jean. "Chateaubriand et Victor Hugo." *Nouvelle Revue de Bretagne* 6 (1952): 254–61, 365–76.

Siccardo, Francesco. "Dante e Victor Hugo." *RLC* 39 (1965): 427–33.

Thibaudet, Albert. "Situation de Victor Hugo." *Revue de Paris* 42 (1935): 258–84.

Valéry, Paul. "Victor Hugo créateur par la forme." *Vues.* Paris: Table Ronde, 1948, pp. 171–81.

Ward, Patricia A. "The Political Evolution of Victor Hugo's Gothic Vision." *MLQ* 34 (1973), 272–82.

———. "Victor Hugo, the Baron von Eckstein and the 'Profondeur des Allemands.' " *RLC* 43 (1969): 459–78.

Works of General Literary History and Criticism

Aubert, Marcel. "Le Romantisme et le Moyen Age." *Le Romantisme et l'art.* Paris: Laurens, 1928.

Baldensperger, Fernand. "Le Genre troubadour." *Etudes d'histoire littéraire.* Vol. 1. Paris: Hachette, 1907.

――――. "Sous le signe de Walter Scott." *RLC* 7 (1927): 47–86.

Burtin, Nicholas. *Un Semeur d'idées au temps de la Restauration, le Baron d'Eckstein.* Paris: Boccard, 1931.

Castex, Pierre-Georges. *Le Conte fantastique en France de Nodier à Maupassant.* Paris: J. Corti, 1951.

Cellier, Léon. *L'Epopée romantique.* Paris: Presses universitaires, 1954.

Challamel, Augustin. *Souvenirs d'un hugolâtre: La Génération de 1830.* Paris: J. Lévy, 1885.

Chard, Alice. *A Dream of Order: The Medieval Ideal in Nineteenth-Century English Literature.* Lincoln: University of Nebraska Press, 1970.

Counson, Albert. *Dante en France.* Erlangen: F. Junge and Paris: Fontemoing, 1906.

Dakyns, Janine R. *The Middle Ages in French Literature 1851–1900.* London: Oxford University Press, 1973.

Doolittle, Dorothy W. "The Relation Between Literature and Medieval Studies in France from 1820–1860." O.P., originally a Ph.D. dissertation, Bryn Mawr, 1933.

Edelman, Nathan. *Attitudes of Seventeenth-Century France Toward the Middle Ages.* New York: Columbia University Press, 1946.

Eggli, Edmond. *Le Débat romantique en France: 1813–1816.* Paris: Les Belles-Lettres, 1933.

Estève, Edmond. "Le Moyen Age dans la littérature du XVIIIe siècle." *Revue de l'Université de Bruxelles* 29 (1923–24): 353–82.

Frankl, Paul. *The Gothic. Literary Sources and Interpretations Through Eight Centuries.* Princeton: Princeton University Press, 1960.

Friederich, Werner P. *Dante's Fame Abroad, 1350–1850.* Rome: Edizioni di Storia e Letteratura, 1950.

Gautier, Théophile. *Histoire du romantisme.* Paris: Charpentier, 1874.

Gleckner, Robert F., and Enscoe, Gerald E., eds. *Romanticism: Points of View.* Englewood Cliffs, N.J.: Prentice-Hall, 1962.

Gossman, Lionel. *Medievalism and the Ideologies of the Enlightenment: The World and Work of La Curne de Sainte-Palaye.* Baltimore: The Johns Hopkins Press, 1968.

Hirsch, E.D., Jr. *Wordsworth and Schelling: A Typological Study of Romanticism.* New Haven: Yale University Press, 1960.

Hunt, Herbert J. *The Epic in Nineteenth-Century France.* Oxford: Blackwell, 1941.

――――. *Le Socialisme et le romantisme en France: Etude de la presse socialiste de 1830 à 1848.* Oxford: Clarendon Press, 1935.

Jacoubet, Henri. *Le Comte de Tressan et les origines du genre troubadour.* Paris: Presses universitaires, 1923.

――――. *Le Genre troubadour et les origines françaises du romantisme.* Paris: Les Belles-Lettres, 1929.

Jensen, Christian A.E. *L'Evolution du romantisme: l'année 1826.* Geneva and Paris: Droz and Minard, 1959.

Kamerbeek, Jan, Jr. *Tenants et aboutissants de la notion "couleur locale."* Utrecht: Instituut voor Algemene Literaturwetenschap, 1962.

Kayser, Wolfgang. *The Grotesque in Art and Literature.* Translated by Ulrich Weisstein. 1963. Reprint. New York: McGraw-Hill, 1966.

Killen, Alice M. *Le Roman terrifiant ou roman noir de Walpole à Anne Radcliffe et son influence sur la littérature française jusqu'en 1840.* Paris: Champion, 1924.

Lanson, René. *Le Goût du moyen âge en France au XVIIIe siècle.* Paris and Brussels: Van Oest, 1926.

Larat, Jean. *La Tradition et l'exotisme dans l'oeuvre de Charles Nodier.* Paris: Champion, 1923.

Lovejoy, A.O. *Essays in the History of Ideas.* 1948. Reprint. New York: Putnam, 1960.

Lukács, Georg. *The Historical Novel.* Translated by Hannah Mitchell and Stanley Mitchell. Boston: Beacon, 1963.

Maigron, Louis. *Le Roman historique à l'époque romantique.* Paris: Hachette, 1898.

———. *Le Romantisme et la mode.* Paris: Champion, 1911.

Milner, Max. *Le Diable dans la littérature française de Cazotte à Baudelaire, 1772–1861.* 2 vols. Paris: J. Corti, 1960.

Monchoux, André. *L'Allemagne devant les lettres françaises de 1814 à 1835.* 2d ed. Paris: A. Colin, 1965.

Moreau, Pierre. *Le Classicisme des romantiques.* Paris: Plon, 1932.

Nagavajara, Chetana. *August Wilhelm Schlegel in Frankreich: Sein Anteil an der Französischen Literaturkritik, 1807–1835.* Tübingen: Niemeyer, 1966.

Peoples, Margaret H. "La Société des Bonnes Lettres (1821–1930)." *Smith College Studies in Modern Languages* 5 (1923): 1–50.

Pevsner, Nikolaus. *Some Architectural Writers of the Nineteenth Century.* Oxford: Clarendon Press, 1972.

Peyre, Henri. *Qu'est-ce que le romantisme?* Paris: Presses universitaires, 1971.

———. "The Originality of French Romanticism." *Symposium* 23 (1969): 333–45.

Salomon, Gottfried. *Das Mittelalter als Ideal in der Romantik.* Munich: Drei Masken, 1922.

Schwab, Raymond. *La Renaissance orientale.* Paris: Payot, 1950

Stallknecht, Newton P., and Frenz, Horst, eds. *Comparative Literature: Method and Perspective.* Carbondale: Southern Illinois University Press, 1961.

Trahard, Pierre. *La Jeunesse de Prosper Mérimée (1803–1834).* Paris: Champion, 1924.

———, ed. *Le Romantisme défini par Le Globe.* Paris: Les Presses françaises, 1924.

Tronchon, Henri. *La Fortune intellectuelle de Herder en France.* Paris: F. Rieder, 1920.

Van Tieghem, Paul. *Ossian en France.* 2 vols. Paris: F. Rieder, 1917.

———. *Le Préromantisme.* 2d ed. 3 vols. Paris: SFELT, 1948.

———. *Le Romantisme dans la littérature européenne.* 1948. Reprint. Paris: Albin Michel, 1969.